FIGHTING CHANCE captu... **ON** ...Regan's life and work. It is a reflection and revelation of real people whose lives were adversely changed through their personal childhood encounters and circumstances and through their pursuit for protection and identity. This book is also a traumatic recall of the never-ending pain felt by families at the murder of a loved one. However this story does not end with tragedy rather it captures the spirit of amazing people whose relentless work amongst young people gives us hope that the darkness of gang culture will be overshadowed by the growing dawn of social enterprise and youth based initiatives.

Reverend Nims Obunge MBE DL Chief Executive, The Peace Alliance/Freedom's Ark

It has never been more important to reach out to young people and make a real difference by offering them opportunities, training and the confidence that could shape and influence their future. Vulnerable youngsters can be easily lured into gangs and criminal activity. Patrick is a shining light in the voluntary sector's efforts to offer young people positive life choices and in ensuring they do not become the unfortunate statistics of tomorrow.

Boris Johnson, Mayor of London

Patrick has created a book which shows a very real picture of the issues facing young people and the problem of gangs today. The use of real-life personal stories provide powerful accounts of the direct effects of gangs and gang activity, which will create a variety of different emotions in the reader. This is a book that everyone, whether they have been directly affected by the issues discussed or not, should pick up and read. Emotional and heartbreaking but very inspirational.

Richard Taylor, Damilola Taylor Trust

In gangs we often see broken people who are hurting. These young men and women seek shelter and identity in gangs partly because they have been told that they will never amount to anything – or that they can have no identity of any worth outside of a gang environment.

My experience, both of inner city life and of a loving creator God, tells me this: such beliefs are totally false. If you tell yourself enough times you cannot do something, and have no worth, it becomes a self-fulfilling prophecy. Our challenge is to bring an end to this by breaking the shackles of self-doubt and worthlessness that entrap our young people into the gang culture.

One way is to encourage our young people to make responsible choices. We need to get alongside young people so they can be the ones transforming our communities for the better. Young people can be inspirational. Young people are not the leaders of tomorrow, they are the leaders of today.

In the aftermath of the murders of Charlene Ellis and Letisha Shakespeare on New Year's Eve 2002, I saw the friends of these girls lead a community in grief, campaign to bring their killers to justice and organise a national tribute to the friends they had lost to gang violence. I still remember their message: 'enough is enough.'

We need to listen to those who have been caught up in gang problems to give us the answer on how to tackle it at the root. God created every single person as a unique individual with infinite worth – and, what's more, God never gives up on us when we get things wrong.

Everywhere I look around I see ordinary people doing amazing things. I see people who care about their communities and their country and want to do something about it. Britain has strong and proud communities, full of wonderful individuals who, sometimes, have not been given a chance to shine. I pay tribute to Patrick Regan, and everyone at XLP, for giving those people in particular a chance to express themselves positively and break the shackles.

Dr John Sentamu, Archbishop of York

I have known Patrick and his work at XLP for a number of years and have great respect for his work amongst the street gangs of London. Patrick's book brings attention to the worrying growth and violence of a lost generation. Anyone who wants to grow in their understanding and skill should read his book as it will increase their knowledge enormously.

Rt Hon Iain Duncan Smith MP, Chairman of the Centre for Social Justice

From the outset, Patrick Regan provides a powerful call to action on gang culture in the UK. Harrowing testimonials from gang members and victims underline that this is too important an issue to ignore. But this is no counsel of despair. FIGHTING CHANCE reminds us that every one of us can make a difference. It shows how, when problems are listened to and acted on, hope can win through.

Rt Hon Stephen Timms MP

Nobody knows or cares more about what is going on along the front lines of our inner cities than Patrick Regan. And nobody is more effective or more passionate than Patrick in persuading others to take actions to end the violence, injury and death. All those who care about Britain's young people should read, mark and learn from Patrick's experience, wisdom and determination to win back our streets for safety and respect.

Simon Hughes MP

In FIGHTING CHANCE, Patrick Regan confronts the complex issues around gang culture head on. He unpicks the practical solutions we miss when through discomfort or embarrassment we shy away from the real questions. Challenging gang culture can present us with uncomfortable truths that too often cause us to stop asking questions at all. This book vocalises the questions that we must keep asking. The personal stories and thoughtful exploration of gang culture form a powerful call to action for every member of our society.

David Lammy MP

The contribution of motivated communities and community leaders in making our cities safer is critical, invaluable and well proven. Patrick Regan is one such leader and continues to show he is insightful, focused and has a real passion and heart for people who may have been pushed into the margins of mainstream life. Yet again, he shows that he is truly in tune with the challenges facing young people and skilfully gets the reader to question their own thoughts, actions and commitment to helping others.

Commander Tony Eastaugh, Metropolitan Police

From violence in the community to growing up without a positive role model in the home – this book examines the multiple causes and offers some robust solutions around the issue of gang culture. A must read for anyone working towards a better future for Britain's disadvantaged youth.

Martina Milburn, Chief Executive of The Prince's Trust

A book that tells the truth about what is going on in gangs, without sensationalism, but most importantly, tells us about the causes. Family breakdowns are at the heart of the problem. Families have to become a big part of the solution.

John Bird MBE, Founder of *The Big Issue*

I believe this book is important because it speaks of an emotive social issue with the authority of experience. It comes from a place of informed compassion, deals with very real and complex challenges facing young people today and looks at what can be done with understanding and with hope. The work of XLP is increasingly far-reaching but not at a cost to local-level commitment. Patrick is highly regarded in political circles and, most importantly, by the countless numbers of young people and their families whose lives have been directly impacted by XLP across London.

Professor Ram Gidoomal CBE, Chairman, South Asian Concern

Fighting Chance

Tackling Britain's Gang Culture

PATRICK REGAN

WITH LIZA HOEKSMA

HODDER

Publisher's Note
Names have been changed throughout in order to protect
the identities of individuals.

First published in Great Britain in 2010 by Hodder & Stoughton
An Hachette UK company

This paperback edition first published in 2011

1

Copyright © Patrick Regan and Liza Hoeksma 2010

A CIP catalogue record for this title is
available from the British Library

ISBN 978 0 340 99632 4

Typeset in AGaramond by Ellipsis Books Limited, Glasgow

Printed and bound in the UK by CPI Mackays, Chatham ME5 8TD

Hodder & Stoughton policy is to use papers that are natural, renewable
and recyclable products and made from wood grown in sustainable
forests. The logging and manufacturing processes are expected to
conform to the environmental regulations of the country of origin.

Hodder & Stoughton Ltd
338 Euston Road
London NW1 3BH

www.hodder.co.uk

Contents

For my Dad: I can't believe what you went through as
I was writing this book. Thanks for never giving up
hope and inspiring me to keep going.

Acknowledgements

Acknowledgements

Patrick would like to thank:
Diane, Keziah, Daniel and Abigail for your patience and support;
Liza for all your hard work and dedication to this project which
went beyond the call of duty;
Simon Hughes for your support in this project;
Joel Edwards for encouraging me to write this book;
The Centre for Social Justice, in particular the *Dying to Belong*
think tank, Charlie Pickles who worked so amazingly hard in
pulling the report together, Simon Antrobus who chaired the
group, and Philippa Stroud for her support.
Diane Louise Jordan – thanks for being a constant source of
encouragement.

Patrick and Liza would like to thank:
The XLP team, especially Anna Bateman, Ethan Bernard, Mike
Biddulph, Charlotte Hansen, Chris Henriette, Simon Marchant,
Leo Pswarayi and Emma Thomas;
everyone who provided comment or case studies and so honestly
shared their stories, including Andy Briers, Dez Brown, CJ, Matt
Collins, Andy Day, David Elliot, Francis, Grace Idowu, Jane,
Laura, Lauren, Ian Levy, Manny, Michael, Nigel, Nyrha, John
Poyton, Sharlene Robinson, Nathaniel Rotimi, Andy Smith, Miss

Lorna Stanley, Stephen, John Sutherland, Terri Lee, Wizdom and GreenJade;

the team at Hodder, especially Wendy Grisham, Joanna Davey and Claire Portal;

Tracey Palmer, Samantha Blowers and Leanne Sedin for reading the manuscript and providing comments and feedback;

Jo Tanner and Kate Perrior at Inhouse PR.

NYRHA'S STORY

I'm the black sheep of my family. My dad is dead, and my mum got a new boyfriend when I was young. She'd disowned me by the time I was eleven. I stopped going to school as I needed money or I wouldn't be able to eat. I was robbing people on the street – it was either that or starve. I'd sleep here and there – or stay out all night doing robberies so I made sure I had enough money for breakfast in the morning.

I first went to prison when I was about fifteen. I thought it was quite funny: I knew everyone there, so it was all right. But since then I've been in and out and it's not so funny any more. You're meant to get help when you get out – it's part of my probation conditions to go and see someone, but they don't do anything so I don't go any more. I might get put back in prison for not going, but at least then I'd have some-where to sleep. At the moment I'm living with my friend's mum. I'm twenty-one. I should be in my own place.

To me, the whole world is bad. I do see people trying to do good, but bad overpowers the good. I've seen people try to get positive and get qualifications, but the recession comes along and they can't get a job. You've got to get money from somewhere, especially when you've got kids to feed. I've got three already, with another on the way.

Guns are easy to get – give me £100 and I'll get you one. Guns are the new fists; it's old school to fight. If trouble starts, someone will just go and get a gun. Even the other night two of my friends were arguing. It was over nothing, but one of them got so mad he went off to get a gun. The guy who was holding it wouldn't give it to him, otherwise he would have shot his own friend.

There's nothing to do around here. We get bored and when we get bored we'll go and look for someone we don't like just for something to do. And the younger generation are worse than us. They're only thirteen or fourteen and they've been at shoot-outs already; it's normal to them. They see it on films and think it looks good, so when there are shots flying around they think they're living in a film. They try and make money so they can get a gun. They get involved with drug dealers. They're living in their own little world. I tell you what, if you put us on an island, we'd have killed each other in five years. There are no rules any more.

I used to be scared of being shot, but now I've been shot and stabbed a few times I'm not scared any more. The only good thing I can see in my life is that I'm still living. When you open your eyes and see what's really going on, you know that life is bad.

Introduction

The fact that you have picked up this book means you care about the rise of gang culture in our country. Gangs are taking lives, devastating communities and crippling us financially by putting ever-increasing pressure on our police, hospitals and justice system. This book is written to help us get a better picture of what is really happening in the lives of young people in gangs, to look behind the headlines and meet some of the individuals involved. It explores the problems and issues leading young people towards such violent lifestyles and helps us understand how such a life can seem appealing. Most significantly, this book will help us explore how we can bring positive change. My hope is that the stories you read here will give you insight, break your heart and inspire you to do something.

What our young people need are individuals who are willing to get involved, to step out of their own world in order to relate to those in a different position. If we are not faced with the violence of gangs on our doorsteps every day it is easy to forget about them, but we need to open our eyes to the state of our society. It is easy to make assumptions and judgements about other people's lives. We can look at violent young teenagers and criticise them for their choices, or we can try to see the world from their perspective. That does not mean we are in any way condoning their actions, but we will never be able to help them if we watch from a distance and simply judge.

President Barack Obama said, 'There's a lot of talk in this country about the federal deficit. But I think we should talk more about the empathy deficit – the ability to put ourselves in someone else's shoes, to see the world through the eyes of those who are different from us. The child who's hungry, the steelworker who's been laid-off, the family who lost the entire life they built together when the storm came to town. When you think like this – when you choose to broaden your ambit of concern and empathise with the plight of others, whether they are close friends or distant strangers – it becomes harder not to act, harder not to help.'

This deficit is not limited to America. Here in the UK we need to understand our young people and then be motivated by empathy for them. We can save ourselves a lot of pain in the future if we are willing to work with young people now, stop pointing fingers and find ways to help them change.

If we do that, we have a fighting chance of turning the situation around.

* * *

DYING TO BELONG

The Centre for Social Justice (CSJ) is an independent think tank that looks for effective solutions to the issues surrounding poverty in the UK. They were concerned, as we were at XLP (see below), about the misunderstandings concerning gangs and recognised that we needed to look into the issues if we were to avoid losing further generations to gangs and gang violence. I was invited to be part of a research team that led to the publication of the 2009 *Dying to Belong* report into gangs. Some of the information in this book comes from our research, including the definition of a gang below.

The definition of a gang

There is much confusion about the term 'gang'. We do not have a standard definition and here lies our first problem in tackling gang culture. A group of young people hanging out on a street corner can sometimes be labelled as a gang, but in reality they are doing what young people love to do – just spending time together. Often there is simply nothing for them to do in their community. They feel they have nowhere to go and so they loiter in groups. This does not mean they are in a gang, or that they are involved in violent crime. There is also a danger of assuming that all youth crime is gang related.

The CSJ working group decided on the following definition and this is what I will use for the purposes of this book:

> A gang is a discernible group of young people who are
> involved in a range of criminal activity and violence, who
> identify with or lay claim over territory, have some form of
> structure (such as a name, a leader, or rules), and are in
> conflict with other gangs.

Glossary of terms

Beef – argument/feud
Crew – gang
Endz – area you live in/territory
Rep – reputation
Elder/Older – leader of a gang
Younger – lower-level gang member
Tiny – very young gang member
Baby – youngest gang member

ABOUT XLP

XLP is about *hope*. It is about getting alongside young people living in our inner cities and helping them see alternatives to what can sometimes seem a hopeless situation. XLP has realised that to see significant change we cannot just offer knee-jerk reactions to problems; if we are to do more than scratch the surface of these complex issues, we need to be committed for the long haul. That is why nearly every week of the year XLP youth workers are tackling issues of educational failure, poverty and deprivation, violence and intimidation, helping young people make wise lifestyle choices and supporting them to realise the amazing potential they have.

XLP began in 1996 after I had been employed as a youth worker in London for a few years. A local school called and asked me to come and speak to their pupils because there had been a stabbing in the playground. This led to regular invitations to take lessons and run assemblies and, as I got to know the young people, I began to see some of the issues they were facing. A friend and I asked people we knew to sponsor us so that we could begin working full time in local schools, supporting young people. That was how XLP was born. The name came from our desire to see kids reach their potential and *excel* in life, hence the XL Project, or XLP as we became known.

Since then XLP has gone from working in one school to having relationships with fifty-seven schools across the London boroughs of Southwark, Lewisham, Greenwich, Bexley, Islington, Camden, Tower Hamlets and Newham. We employ over twenty full-time members of staff, have up to sixty volunteers working on projects at any one time and have over twenty students each year who are trained through our 'gap year' programme. XLP is a Christian charity that is faith-based but not faith-biased. We work equally with young people of all faiths and none.

Educational support

We run regular clubs and have a portfolio of support sessions that include citizenship and religious education lessons, lunchtime activity clubs, homework support, music, drama, art, playground youth work, in-class behavioural and educational support, and study and skills clubs.

XL-R8 Project

We also work on a number of estates using both community facilities and our own double-decker buses that are equipped with computers with internet access, facilities for arts and crafts, and a 'chill-out area'. The buses provide a safe place for children and young people to engage in positive activities and learn outside school hours.

We also run a number of specific projects you will read more about in this book.

Gunz Down is an hour-long multimedia show we take into schools alongside hip hop group GreenJade, to address the issues around young people carrying guns and knives. Follow-up lessons are also offered so that the issues can be explored further.

Arts Showcases offer a platform for young people to articulate the challenges they face using their chosen art form. At the same time they can show their talent to families, friends, teachers and the wider community. Auditions are held in schools, and are followed by rehearsals and vibrant shows that allow students to explore their potential in the performing arts. We also use our state-of-the-art mobile recording studio to work with young people on their estate and within their schools, giving them the chance to record and produce music.

COACH (Creating Opportunities And Casting Hope) is one of our most recent initiatives and is run with the Catalyst Trust. It formalises the mentoring we have found to be vital in supporting young people who are at risk of exclusion and gang life. Volunteer mentors meet with a young person each week for a year to help them improve their life skills, relate better to their peers and community, avoid educational failure and choose not to become involved with gangs.

Our aims

We want to see young people with:

- a raised sense of self-worth and self-esteem and increased educational achievement which helps them to contribute confidently and positively to society;
- fresh goals and the desire to work hard to achieve them, and an ability to make wise lifestyle choices;
- positive attitudes and behaviours towards their communities, their families, peers, local residents, teachers and the police.

You can read more about the history of XLP in our book *Conspiracy of the Insignificant* (Kingsway, 2007) and find out more about the work of XLP at www.xlp.org.uk.

Part One

How Did We Get Here?

1

A Warning for Our Future

Have you any idea what it's like to walk into your brother's bedroom and see him swimming in a pool of his own blood? Do you have any idea how it feels to walk in and see him struggle for one breath? Do you have any idea how it feels to watch your brother suffocate on his own collar bone because some idiot ran into our house and shot him? My little brother who was gonna grow up and look after us – gone. For what? SE15, SW9. What's that? A couple of numbers? A couple of letters of the alphabet?

We the youth – each one of us – has the potential to grow up and change this world. So if you're telling me that 'us' – the future – are stabbing each other and going in each other's houses and shooting each other, taking lives like we can give it back – tell me this – what kind of future are we gonna be?

These powerful words were spoken by Rachel and Sharlene, two girls living in a community devastated by the murder of an innocent fifteen-year-old boy, Michael Dosunmu. Two men burst into Michael's house in search of his older brother, who they believed owed them money. In a case of mistaken identity they shot Michael, a church-going schoolboy, as he slept in his bed.

Sadly this is not a stand-alone case. The media is full of high-profile stabbings and shootings, many of which are gang related, and the violence is getting worse. What was once happening under the cover of darkness now takes place in broad daylight – a man being stabbed in the head outside a huge and busy supermarket at 5 p.m., a shooting in a McDonald's in the middle of the day. The stories are shocking and so are the facts.

- In the past five years there has been an 89 per cent increase in the number of under-sixteens admitted to hospital with serious stab wounds and a 75 per cent increase in older teenagers.[1]
- The percentage of schoolchildren who carry a knife increased by more than 50 per cent between 2002 and 2005.[2]
- The Metropolitan and Strathclyde Police have both identified 170 gangs in their areas. This could equate to about five thousand gang members in each area. The actual figures are likely to be a lot higher, as these are just the gangs known to the police.
- In Manchester and Liverpool around 60 per cent of shootings are gang related.
- Glasgow has at least a hundred gangs according to Strathclyde Police. In Easterhouse alone there are fourteen gangs in six square miles.
- Police say there has been a 500 per cent increase in the number of children taking some kind of weapon to school.[3] They also acknowledge that their statistics on knife crime do not take into account the number of stabbings that take place using another sharp instrument (such as the recent trend to use the sharp edge of a broken CD to inflict serious damage).

The figures are stark and this rise in violence caused one national newspaper to display a death counter on its front page. Dramatic and attention grabbing, maybe, but the trouble is that a death toll (along with just looking at statistics) dehumanises the whole problem of gangs and gang-related deaths. This is a real issue in our country and I am passionate that we all take some responsibility for it and really try to get to grips with what is going on. As Gandhi said, we must be a part of the change we wish to see. Rather than sitting on the sidelines and making judgements about other people's lives, if we are to have any hope of turning this around we must be willing to get our hands dirty. We must take ownership of our communities so that the problems faced by the community become *our* problems. Too often we approach communities who are struggling by going and doing something *to* them or *for* them. We may have the best intentions, but that is not what is needed. People want us to understand what they are facing and take action *with* them.

We need to understand who the people behind the headlines are, see what the real problems are, and find out what would drive a young person into a life of violence and crime so that we can reach out to them.

The press do not always give us the full picture either. You might remember the tragic killing of eleven-year-old Rhys Jones in Liverpool. He too was the innocent victim of mistaken identity and his violent death certainly deserved the coverage it received. But just a few weeks later one of the XLP team was working in a Lewisham school when a pupil broke down in tears. As it turned out, her cousin had been stabbed to death in Peckham Rye a few days before. No matter how hard we searched, my team and I could not find a single news report of this equally tragic death. It didn't even make the local news. There seems to be no rhyme or reason as to why one story is splashed across the media for days and another not even mentioned, but it is clear that we are not given the full picture of what is happening.

There is also a danger that through the media all young people become stereotyped. When the vast majority of news stories we hear about teenagers involve violence, crime and drugs, it does not take long before people start to associate that kind of behaviour with all teenagers. Of course not every teenager belongs to a gang or behaves in a criminal or violent way, but the stories reported are the sensational ones and they create a fear of teenagers. This fear enhances the divide between adults and young people. It is difficult for the teenagers who make good choices and stay away from criminal activity to see these reports as they may feel they are tarred with the same brush. It frustrates me that truly positive stories are very rarely told. Plenty of teenagers face tough situations but stay away from gangs, guns and crime, yet no one seems to want to talk about them.

Often situations get blown out of proportion by the press causing 'Ban the Hoodie'-type campaigns that completely miss the point. It is easy to label a group and blame them, but the issues are much more complex. Clearly not everyone who wears a hoodie is carrying a weapon and belongs to a gang. Sadly, many young people do get caught up in gangs, but instead of looking at stereotypes, we need to explore why young people often turn to violence. We need to find out why so many are full of anger and what it is that drives them into gangs.

Since I started XLP in 1996, I have been living in south-east London where a lot of the issues are on my doorstep, sometimes literally. In one of the first houses my wife Diane and I lived in, right in the heart of Peckham, there was a group of brothers and sisters living next door and they were part of a gang. Sometimes our walls would shake if things were kicking off in their house. The gang would often hang around outside our front door with their pit bull terrier (nicknamed Kill). The Elder was a big Nigerian guy who was incredibly polite to us, but when he was not around the Youngers would sometimes give us trouble, even shouting at my mum as she tried to get into our house. The Elder would apologise to us for the others, but we knew he was not a man to be messed with – I overheard him threaten to kill someone if they did not get him the money he was owed. Often the gang would be smoking weed, but whenever we asked them to stop, they would. Regardless, it was not the nicest thing in the world to have people dealing drugs right by our house, particularly when we had a six-month-old baby girl.

Through the work of XLP in schools we have become very aware of the rise of gun and knife crime. One of the situations that really made me realise how serious things were getting in London was when I was away speaking at a youth event. I phoned home to speak to Diane and could hear police sirens in the background, as well as my daughter crying because she had been woken by the sounds of gunshots. I knew we had to do something. I spoke to some friends of mine who are in a hip hop band called GreenJade. Like me, they were feeling that the situation was getting out of control and there had to be something we could do. Wizdom from GreenJade told me they had been performing at a New Year's Eve party in Birmingham a few months before, when Letisha Shakespeare and Charlene Ellis were shot on the streets nearby. You might remember their story, which was splashed across the media for days. Both girls were simply in the wrong place at the wrong time when bullets meant for rival gang members hit them instead. Two lives were taken. Two families were left without a daughter, a sister, a niece, a cousin. And two circles of friends were devastated by the tragic loss.

So GreenJade and I were in agreement that we had to try something to get across anti-gun and knife messages to young people.

Anything to stop these senseless deaths. We came up with the idea of a tour called *Gunz Down* that we would take into schools. The tour is basically a show that puts across how to make good choices in a really engaging way. Through music, drama and rap we unpack how you can 'talk down' a situation rather than letting it escalate to the point where someone gets hurt. We mainly took it to schools where we were already working so that we could continue to build on these themes, getting to know the young people and helping them see that they do have choices.

Through *Gunz Down* we met individuals like fifteen-year-old Rakeem, who approached us wearing a bulletproof vest under his school uniform. At first we thought he was messing around, but we soon realised his fear was genuine when we heard that his cousin had been shot, his brother was lying in hospital and he had been told that a rival gang wanted to kill him. The *Gunz Down* show gave him an opportunity to be honest with us about how bad things had become in his life and how he had found himself in serious trouble. We found Rakeem a mentor and he was doing really well at staying away from trouble, but six weeks later he was stabbed when leaving school one afternoon. The knife went in millimetres from his central nervous system and he only narrowly escaped serious injury.

The team and I were deeply impacted by Rakeem's story. He was alive for now, but if things were like this for him at fifteen, where would his future take him? How many others like him would not make it? How many schoolchildren would see one of their friends or classmates stabbed in broad daylight?

It was around this time that I was approached by The Centre for Social Justice to take part in their research into gangs. The report *Dying to Belong* involved a team of thirteen, including youth work practitioners, academics, government policy advisors, people who work in prisons and CEOs of other charities, working together for fourteen months. We listened to young people, community leaders, the police, schoolteachers, and many grassroots organisations working in urban areas in different parts of the UK, to get one of the first accurate understandings of the scale of problem, so that we could recommend policy changes. Some of the statistics in this book come from that report, but my passion is that we see behind the figures, beyond numbers and percentages, and find out what is really going on in the lives of the kids those numbers represent. Every statistic is a life. Every single one represents someone's child, someone's friend, someone's schoolmate, someone's neighbour.

A STARK WARNING FOR THE FUTURE

As part of the Centre for Social Justice report, members of the working group also travelled to other countries to understand different aspects of gang culture and to learn from the people who are tackling it. I was part of a group that went to Los Angeles in California, which is known as the gang capital of the world. Some areas have over five active gangs for every square mile – that is as many as sixty-eight gangs in one town. It is estimated that there are one hundred and fifty thousand gang members in the area in total, with notorious gangs like The Crips having around thirteen thousand members in LA[4] as well as other sets in different areas of California and further afield. Gangs are incredibly institutionalised, with many born into families where their dad and grandad have been gang leaders. The assumption and the fact is that their children will grow up to take on that leadership themselves.

Language and colours have become extremely important, with gang members going to excessive lengths to identify themselves with their crew. The Crips are known for wearing blue and their rivals, the Bloods, for wearing red. Neither would ever be seen wearing a scrap of their rivals' colour. Their language has been developed to back up their gang associations and they avoid certain letters – for example, the Crips will not write 'ck' as this stands for 'Crip Killer', so they use 'cc' instead. The Bloods will not use the letter 'c' at all, so will pick up a 'bup of boffee' instead of a cup of coffee. Gangs are also easily spotted by their tattoos, which identify which crew they are with. Some girls even have '666' tattooed on their stomachs.

Graffiti is commonly used to mark out territory and show domination of an area. Anyone living in that area can then become a target for a rival gang, whether they have any affiliation or not, and many innocent people get caught up in the fighting. Gangs also use commonly understood codes and symbols in their graffiti to challenge their rivals and show their power or status.

When we met with the Los Angeles Police Department (LAPD) they told us that someone is shot almost every day and in 2007 there was a gang-related murder in LA every other day. Their problems are clearly far ahead of our current situation in the UK, but they have valuable lessons for us. For example, there are gangs in London who call themselves 'Bloods' and 'Crips' and keep with the gang colours of their American equivalents, showing how young people here are looking up to and emulating the violence over there. The LAPD showed us graphic, stomach-turning images, like a video of a four-year-old girl who was caught in the crossfire of a drive-by shooting and killed. They told us that even locking up gang leaders does not seem to help; the leaders are just as powerful in prison as out of it and can control whole areas from their cell. We visited one of LA's poorest areas and parts of the city where kids cannot walk freely because gangs have claimed different neighbourhoods as 'territories'. In case we had not realised how serious this was, we were shown a middle school with four exit points. Children are only allowed to leave by the specific exit that leads to their home area: if they leave by another there could be life-threatening consequences.

There are, of course, people working to change things and there are signs of hope. The mayor of Los Angeles created an Office of Gang Reduction and Youth Development which identifies areas most affected by gangs. They map their needs and target specific support to these areas, such as increasing police presence and running prevention, intervention and reinforcement programmes. Individuals are making a difference too. We met a Christian couple, Scott and Sarah, who, along with their two children and six volunteers, moved into a particularly violent area of the city. Some communities within inner-city LA are very fragmented: people keep themselves to themselves and do not know the people living in their own community, let alone look to help them. Scott and Sarah wanted to model something different and show people what genuine community can look like. They open up their home, invite people to come and have meals with them and use the base-ment of their house as a youth centre where kids can hang out and do graffiti together. They are so generous with everything they have that there are always people coming and going and their kindness has significantly impacted those around them, many of whom have never had such considerate and thoughtful neighbours before. I was intrigued to find that the houses up and down their road are protected by great thick bars at the windows – and the only house without them is the one belonging to Scott and Sarah. Amazingly, they do not need the protection as the community respects them so much that they've never had any trouble.

While Scott was showing us around the community, we passed a large mural. Along the top were the names of murdered gang members, and underneath the names were scenes from the last days of Jesus' life. It seemed as though the suffering of Christ was something that the artists could identify with. The first name on the list was Nightowl. Scott told me he knew Nightowl's brother Hector well, as they had shared a flat together. One night Hector's dad asked him to find Nightowl, Hector delayed for some reason and that night Nightowl was shot. The dad blamed Hector for Nightowl's death. Hector, as a reaction to his brother's death, got more deeply involved in drugs and crime and started carrying a gun. Today, however, Hector no longer lives that lifestyle. With encouragement and support from Scott, Hector became a Christian and now goes back into communities to help vulnerable young people get out of that lifestyle.

It was so inspiring to see a family putting into practice what many only talk about – moving into an area so they could truly reach the people there and be in community with them. They were willing to go to any lengths to make a difference and it really pays off when you hear stories of people like Hector who have turned their whole lives around as a result.

One thing the authorities in LA told us repeatedly was that the UK is not yet in the same situation, as the gangs in LA are much more institutionalised. However, time and time again we heard the same warning: the signs in the UK are the same as they were in LA a number of years ago. Unless we act quickly, engage young people who are at risk of getting involved in gangs and address the things that push them towards it, then we will end up in the same situation they are facing on the West Coast of America. If we do not get involved now, the situation will get worse and gangs here will become a part of life that we are powerless to stop. We will see more and more young people's lives taken from them in violence.

We can all do something about this situation.

We all have a part to play.

We must act now.

2

What Is Going On?

In the space of a weekend, we had eleven different
shootings. That was Friday to Sunday – one was a fatality,
others were serious injuries. All young people, all gang-
related – and one guy literally shot himself in the foot.
(*Dr Derrick Campbell, Chief Executive of Race
Equality, Birmingham*)

It is almost impossible to put a figure on the number of young
people involved in gangs. After all, they are hardly likely to want
to identify themselves to those in authority, given what they are
getting up to. That said, those who do speak up may well boast
about having larger numbers than they actually do in order to
magnify their status. It is often the case that gangs at their core are
not huge, but they have lots of young people who affiliate themselves with the group. If there is a major disagreement or beef
between one area and another, that is when those affiliated to the
gang will get involved.

The most recent estimates put the figure of those in gangs at
twenty thousand young people in England and Wales,[1] but this
was based only on those aged over seventeen and, as we will go on
to discuss further in chapter 3, gang members are often well below
this age. The decrease in age has meant that for future reports the
British Crime Survey will begin to include under-sixteens in order

to truly reflect the current situation.[2] If London and Strathclyde Police have each identified 170 gangs in their area, and these are only the ones they know about, the implication is that the figures could be much higher than twenty thousand in total.

Worryingly, the evidence suggests that gangs are not only increasing in number, but are also becoming more violent and members are far more likely to carry a knife or a gun than in previous generations. As one community worker in Birmingham commented, 'A gun is easier to get now than a mobile phone.' This may have been an exaggeration to make a point, but in a number of the conversations I have had with young people in the course of writing this book, they have said they could get a gun right there and then. The huge increase in knife and gun crime also speaks for itself.

The Chair of the National Independent Advisory Group (appointed by the Association of Chief Police Officers) said that guns are too readily available and that, 'We would have had a lot more deaths on our streets if it wasn't for the fact that the youngsters firing the guns are such poor shots – people are shot in the leg, in the back, wherever. And there are a lot of injuries that are just not reported.'

Through the work of XLP in schools, we have seen evidence of this increase in gang violence too. In fact, as I said earlier, I started the charity in 1996 after being invited to speak in a school that was reeling from a stabbing in the playground. Since then we have been taking lessons, holding the *Gunz Down* tour I mentioned in the previous chapter, encouraging pupils to express themselves through dance, drama, comedy, rap and song in our Arts Showcase events, and running lunch clubs. In one instance we were due to go into a Peckham school to run a lunchtime club and found that the school had been evacuated under the threat of an attack from a gang. The previous week, tension between Lewisham's Ghetto

Boys and the Peckham Boys had resulted in the stabbing and death of a twenty-nine-year-old man. The gang wanted revenge for this killing and were planning to ambush their rivals when they left school. Thankfully, the police received a tip-off so were able to send the 700 pupils home early while they stood guard at the school. It shocked us as a team, since we had never heard of a school being evacuated in that way before.

This is an indication of how the vicious downward spiral of violence continues. Someone is killed and so the gang want revenge. They kill one of their rivals in retaliation, so that gang want revenge for the revenge killing. It is a never-ending cycle of death and violence.

You do not have to be an active member of any gang to get caught up in all this, either. If you happen to live on an estate that has a well-known gang, you can be seen by their rivals as belonging to that gang. As Professor John Pitts, author of *Reluctant Gangsters*,[3] puts it, 'residency becomes synonymous with affiliation', making many young people targets just because of where they live.

Daniel, a youth worker and former gang member, says the gang situation is much worse than when he was younger. He says that gangs are much more serious now, holding strongly onto the identity and name of their crew. They are more organised and getting smarter at how to avoid the police, changing their mobile phones every few weeks so that they cannot be traced. 'Back in my day there were the guys in gangs, some who knew them and then people who were outside the whole thing. Now if you're not in a clique you're a target so you'll get beaten up and robbed. You'd better be identified with someone to avoid it.'

Daniel says that old codes of conduct have also gone out of the window with this generation. 'In my day if you were in an argument with someone and saw they had their little brother or sister with them, then you'd know they'd need to get them home and you'd leave it for then.'

'That can't save you no more,' says Joe, one of the young people we work with who is currently trying to get out of the gang lifestyle. 'I was with my four-year-old cousin, sat on the back of the bus, and these guys started. They tried it with me but I'd never have done that when little family members were there. That won't stop anyone any more.'

TERRITORIES

One of the most terrifying developments in gang culture has been the development of 'postcode wars'. At one time the identity of a gang was centred around ethnicity, but now, while it may be true that in Glasgow gangs tend to be white and in Brixton they are more likely to be African-Caribbean, identity is based on where you live. If you come from SE15 (Peckham), you can literally be risking your life by going to SW9 (Brixton); if you are from S3 in Sheffield, then S5 is a no-go area, and so it goes on. It seems as if the areas being fought over are getting smaller and smaller. I have seen this happen in Jamaica where there was a main road that divided gang territory. On my next visit, just a few years later, gangs had started to control different blocks, meaning gang members could not walk to streets that were within a stone's throw of where they lived for fear of reprisal. One of my friends out there, Destruction, could not even attend the funeral of a good friend of his because the service was being held in a different block that would not be safe. As more gangs spring up over here, we are in danger of similar situations where they are fighting over smaller and smaller areas.

The crazy thing is that no one knows how it started or why different postcodes became rivals. As Joe told me, 'I'm from New

Cross and there's no way I'd go into Peckham. They'd try to move to me [sic]. You know people's faces and you know who's from your area and who isn't. I don't know how it started. I was born into it and just grew up in it. You're continuing the fight but you don't know what you're fighting for. The kids don't know nothing – they're following Olders who only know a little bit.'

Gangs protect their turf by any means necessary. In 2008 Henry Bolombi, aged eighteen, was stabbed to death in Edmonton. One of his friends said, 'It wasn't an organised fight, they just saw them in their area and that's when beef happens. It's just the way it is. They just don't like each other and when you see one of them in your area they better get out because otherwise there is going to be trouble. He was caught up in that.'[4]

For charities like XLP who are trying to reach young people, the postcode wars are a nightmare in more ways than one. We run Arts Showcases four times a year in four London boroughs with the aim of encouraging young people to express themselves through music and performance. Generally they are brilliant evenings with a fantastic atmosphere as family and friends come along and support the acts and are amazed at the talent on display. But we have also had situations where a gang have heard that a member of a rival gang is going to be at our showcase and have brought their crew down for a fight. We have had to call the police to ensure every-one's safety and smuggle performers out of the venue so that no one comes after them. It was very strange for us as a team to see some of the consequences of the postcode wars so close up. We often hear about these situations, but unless we really engage in the issues we do not realise how where they live can really affect so many young people. At the time we felt very vulnerable, but in some ways it made us more determined to make our showcases events that continue to address these issues, and we have worked hard to make sure that people are safe at our shows.

As an extension of the arts project, we set up a recording studio at our offices in Lewisham to help mentor young people and give them a voice through music. What we had not taken into account was the fact that lots of people would not come and use the facility because it was not safe for them to be in the area. We realised we needed to be able to be mobile, so we approached MTV and asked them to do a special *Pimp My Ride* programme. They agreed and teamed up with EMI to turn an old police riot van into a mobile recording studio so that we could cross territories and postcodes, reaching the young people where they feel safe. In the same way, rather than having one youth centre where we expect kids to come to us, we have found the best thing to do is to take a bus onto different estates after school. The upstairs is fitted out with laptops where young people can come and do their homework, particularly if they are from a family that cannot afford a computer at home. Downstairs is like a youth centre with games consoles and *Guitar Hero*. The bus creates a safe place that young people can use without fear and means we are going onto their turf rather than always expecting them to come to us.

As one of the guys who uses our bus, Khan, said, 'The gang stuff has turned into a territory thing, people stick to their own endz and their own postcode. Truthfully, if I weren't with XLP and other youth clubs, I would be doing the same thing I was doing a long time ago – hanging out on the streets and getting nicked.'

DRUGS

Predictably, some of the territory wars are about drugs. A 2004 Offending, Crime and Justice Survey found that 45 per cent of gang members had used drugs in the previous twelve months. Even those who do not use drugs see it as an easy way to make money. Estimates of a gang member's drugs earnings are around £130,000 a year. To make money you have to 'own' the drugs trade in your area, so you have to be prepared to defend your turf if someone else tries to sell drugs there. It is usually left to the younger gang members to protect the market, which often results in violent clashes. The gangs think they own everything in their area and their attitude is that no one can come to their area and do something they do not like. It comes down to protecting your area and so protecting your reputation.

RESPECT

Reputation and respect have become huge motivators in gang violence in recent years. Where so many young people are craving status and a sense of belonging, gangs have become a place to find those things that are missing from their lives. Gangs can also create a sense of excitement and just by being part of one someone might begin to feel respected and popular.

As in most situations, respect has to be earned and on the streets it is usually earned through showing that you do not care about authority, stealing, beating people up, taking risks and proving how tough you are. Once someone has earned themselves a rep, they are desperate to hold on to it. Joe said, 'My mum sent me to Jamaica to live with my dad for a couple of weeks 'cos I was in so much trouble, but when I came back I started terrorising everyone. My name was flowing around the area so I had to keep that up. I started beating people on their hands with a belt and they were too scared to stop me so my name went all over. I was only fourteen then.'

'Dissing' someone, or showing them disrespect, is now justifiable cause to start a fight or a beef. If a gang member feels that someone has given them a funny look or made a disrespectful remark, it can start untold amounts of trouble. As Joe said, 'That's how it is: it happens every day and I'm not even looking to start no trouble. People start beef over that, just a look, 'cos they just want an excuse to start. They want to say they beat someone up.' It is believed that the 2007 murder of fourteen-year-old Martin Dinnegan was due to a 'dirty look', as was the stabbing of sixteen-year-old Nassirudeen Osawe in Islington the same year. The more it happens, the more everyone becomes paranoid about someone disrespecting them. They do not want someone to start on them as it looks bad for their rep, so they are quick to start on that person instead.

So many of these young people are trying to prove themselves, to show how hard they are and to show that they do not care, even if they do. Joe said, 'You know it's wrong. You say you're hard, "I'm gonna be heartless", but you're not. You're just trying to be heartless. You try to justify it by going [sic] heartless, proving you're the hardest to everyone in the area. You rob that guy to prove yourself to others, then you think you're not a waste, but you are. You don't wanna believe you're a wasteman.'

Even in individual gangs, members will start on each other to get respect. Whereas a few years ago Youngers would have respected the Elders, now they know that if they take them on they can gain a rep for themselves. As Elijah (from whom we will hear more later) put it, 'By the time I was fifteen . . . I couldn't show any signs of weakness . . . if you show weakness the one below you will take over. This one guy hated me 'cos I used to boss him around and make him feel small, like he's nothing. If he'd had a chance he would have overthrown me – probably killed me – and the others would have backed him as he would be the one in power. I would have done the same to the person above me. I was about fifteen.'

There's a brilliant film called *The Freedom Writers* which tells the amazing true story of a teacher in Los Angeles called Erin Gruwell, who works with a class full of gang members. In one scene a pupil from the class says to Erin, 'When you die for your own you die with respect.' Erin replies, 'When you die you are going to rot in the ground and people are going to go on living and forget all about you. And when you rot do you think it's going to matter that you were an original gangster? You're dead.' It is a cold truth. This 'respect' that is being fought for on our streets, that many young people think is worth dying for, actually means nothing once someone is dead and buried. But if it is life and death to them, we cannot ignore it. We have to see why street code says that it is better to be respected than loved. We have to understand just who is being drawn into this lifestyle and what is pushing them towards it.

ELIJAH'S STORY

I was only six years old when my dad attacked my mum with a knife. He was sent to prison for seven years; I didn't want to see him, but my mum told me I had to. I had to travel for hours to get there. I was so young and it was really frightening as a kid being in the same room as all these scary guys. It was a lot of stress to deal with and on top of that I had a speech problem which made it hard for me to make myself understood. No one would listen to me because they didn't know what I was saying; they'd talk to my sister instead. My frustrations and anger came out as violence. I got into so many fights at school that I got excluded when I was just eight years old. A couple of years later a boy made what I thought was a racist comment about me and I went mad and beat him until he bled. I got excluded again. I loved football and was playing for Charlton when I was in primary school, but I attacked the referee after he made a decision I didn't like and I got kicked off the programme. I always sorted my problems out with my fists; I didn't know any other way.

We moved to Deptford when I was nine and during my first week I got beaten up. The guy was four years older than me and the only thing that provoked him was the fact that I was from Peckham. He gave me a black eye. Not long after that another guy came up to me and said, 'Do you want to be my Younger? No one will touch you if you are.' That sounded good to me, so I was recruited into his gang and no one got rude any more.

There was a real sense of family in the group – I knew right from the start that they looked after their own and I wouldn't get touched by anyone else. There were about three hundred in the gang in total, but around thirty Youngers like me in my area. It gave me a real sense of power and security being a part of it. Every time my mum let me out I'd go and hang out with them. We'd play *Pro Evo*™ on the PlayStation, rob shops, play fight and beat random people up just for something to do.

It wasn't long, though, 'til I wanted revenge for the fact that I had been beaten up just 'cos of where I came from. I started intimidating people in school and on the streets, threatening them with knives. I even threatened to shoot them, but I didn't actually have a gun. I wanted money, so I stole from people. I wanted to hurt them too, but I didn't want to shoot anyone. The gang told me to take a gun, but I thought that would make me weak. I figured if I could kill someone with a knife and they had a gun, then that made me better than them. And I didn't want to get five years in prison just for holding a gun.

One day at school I was mocking my headteacher when she came up behind me and heard it all. She told me I'd never make it to Year 9. I was so angry that I got a group of mates together. I got one guy to bring petrol and I got some matches – I was so angry I wanted to burn the school to the ground. My mate didn't quite get it though – he brought oil instead of petrol, so of course it wouldn't light. One of the teachers saw what I was trying to do, so I got excluded for two weeks anyway. When I went back it wasn't long before I was in trouble again. Someone in my French class cussed my mum, so I hit him with a table. I was kicked out for another two weeks. I was scared to tell my mum I'd been excluded again, but I soon got over it. While I was off I just played PlayStation and invited my mates round who bunked school, so it wasn't exactly a hard punishment.

It was Year 9 when I got permanently excluded. One of the teachers had been keeping me and some mates in detention after school and I got into an argument with him. For some reason he said he'd squash my mum; I wouldn't let anyone cuss her, so I went to leave and one of my mates hit him. I didn't want to hit a teacher – to me it was the same as hitting a girl so I just wouldn't do it, but I got kicked out anyway.

I was sent to a Pupil Referral Unit, which we all called 'Centre'. It was supposed to help me carry on with my education, but I didn't do any work at first. The teachers were scared of us so they never made us do anything. We'd just go on the internet when we were supposed to be doing maths and we never got stopped. What I really liked doing was playing football and after a while at the centre I put together a team. I started acting good for a bit, but then this guy from outside school said he wanted to stab me and was going to come after me. I thought I'd stab him first so I brought a knife in with me the next day, but before I saw him I saw the Head of Key Stage 3. We got into an argument and he was really annoying me so I thought I'd stab him too. One of the teachers I really liked got in the way and stopped me doing it. The Head asked for my knife, which I gave him, but I got kicked out of the centre as well as getting sent to court. I got a caution and was given a youth worker to try and help me.

There were a few teachers who liked me at the centre and

they fought for me to come back, so I was put on a one-month trial. During that time I had to meet one to one with my youth worker in the library. He'd help me do the work I was supposed to be doing, plus we'd talk about what had happened, how I could have handled things differently and how I was going to cope with similar situations when I went back to the other classroom. I had some good days and some bad days. I was a nice person 'til my pride got hurt, then I'd get into fights. If I was in an argument, people would say to me, 'You can't let him say that,' so I felt like I had to respond and I'd get into it and hurt them, but I managed to stay out of trouble enough to get kept on at the end of the month.

By the time I was fifteen everyone in my area knew me – for all the wrong reasons. I didn't care about anything. I didn't take school stuff seriously so I was acting bad; I'd be rude to the teachers and did stuff like start food fights. My mum still reckoned I was a good person – she saw potential in me, but my anger let me down. I knew I couldn't kill someone, there's no way my mum would accept that, but I would stab people and wouldn't care. I didn't even feel guilty. I didn't regret anything. I would just think, 'I stabbed him or fought him 'cos he deserved it.' To 'deserve it' all someone had to do was be from a different area and be caught on their own. A lot of people ended up in hospital because of how badly I beat them up; the rest of the gang were the same – beating people up, stabbing and shooting them.

I couldn't show any signs of weakness to anyone in the gang. When you're one of the lower people no one cares what you do, but when you get to a certain level, where you're in charge of others your age – if you show weakness the one below you will take over. This one guy hated me 'cos I used to boss him around and make him feel small, like he's nothing. If he'd had a chance he would have overthrown me – probably killed me – and the others would have backed him as he would be the one in power. I would have done the same to the person above me.

When I was in Year 11, I was given a mentor again as I was in so much trouble and I was close to getting kicked out of the centre permanently. His name was Chris and my first thought was, 'Why is this idiot talking to me? He's got no status.' I cursed him and my teachers. My teachers said I wouldn't get a pass in my exams, but I actually got a merit so I just thought, 'You idiots can't say nothing to me. You haven't gone through what I've gone through. You don't know anything.' Me and my mate Moses ruled the place and we really threw our weight around. We'd run out of class if we wanted to or just throw paper at the teachers until they called the Head in. All the other kids were scared of us and we threatened them so that they'd vote for us to be things like Footballer of the Year when it came to awards. The teachers were amazed if we were ever quiet and gave us tokens for the tuck shop just for that.

I didn't even behave in church. My mum is a Reverend and I was brought up in a Pentecostal church, but I thought I was God. I beat up this boy in a church service for looking at me dodgy, but the ushers pulled me off. The pastor was telling me to calm down, but that made me even madder; I didn't want anyone telling me what to do so I attacked him. The police got called, but the pastor said he didn't want to press charges because he thought we should settle it between ourselves. But it made me think no one could touch me; I felt like I must be God if I could get away with attacking the pastor. None of the youth workers could get through to me; the only person who could calm me down was my sister. I thought my mum was weak and I didn't have that much respect for her because she wanted me to keep in touch with my dad even though he'd stabbed her. But my sister, she was my role model and she'd make me realise when I'd done something I shouldn't have. She used to pray for me every night, though, and that made me so angry. I wanted to hit her, wanted her to give up on me.

I hated Christians. They always seemed to be happy and I never was. Even when I was laughing and joking around I wasn't happy. That's why I hurt a lot of people. If I saw people smiling I'd think, 'What right do they have?' I never smiled. I didn't even get it when people cried over something that happened to one of their friends. Mine had been shot and I never cried. So I asked them about it and they said they loved their friends; I didn't even like any of mine. If one of them had been killed I would have looked for revenge, but I wouldn't have cared about them dying. I didn't have a bond with them. We were protecting each other, but there was no real relationship there. I couldn't relax and be myself.

Eventually I started listening to Chris – mainly because I realised he knew some people I knew and I thought they were decent, so I thought he must be all right too. He helped me finish some of my work and helped me out with football by getting me trials with Wayne Rooney's *Street Striker* competition and the TV show *Football Icon*. When I broke my Achilles tendon in a match I obviously couldn't play any more, but Chris kept calling me and checking I was all right. He helped me apply to colleges and took me all the way over to Richmond to see the college there, even though it was two hours from where he worked, because he knew my mum couldn't take me. I was scared to open my mouth at the interview because I was sure I'd start swearing and stuff, so Chris spoke to them for me. I needed pretty high grades to get in and I just thought there was no way it would happen, even though Chris gave me a great reference and persuaded the Head to as well. I started acting bad again, going mental 'cos I thought I hadn't got it. I was mouthing off in class, running around the school, not doing my work or not even turning up some days. Chris kept telling me I'd get in, but I wouldn't listen, I just couldn't believe it would happen for me. When the college came back to me they said yes, they wanted me!

Being in college really calmed me down; I wasn't violent or anything. I wasn't being bad any more – I didn't even have time to see my gang 'cos of the travel to and from college. They gave me a bit of hassle, but then some rumours started that I'd gone to prison so I got left alone more after that. I didn't miss any of them. Everyone else at the college was calm so there was no need for me to be how I used to be. I stayed in touch with Chris, he'd call me to see how college was and I realised how much sense he'd been talking. He'd told me you could resolve confrontations by talking and turning the other cheek, but I hadn't believed him. Now I got it and if someone started on me I wouldn't rise to it. That stopped others from starting as I wasn't getting involved. I remembered hitting this boy before and he wouldn't hit me back. He kept saying, 'I'm better than that,' which just made me more and more angry. He was a Christian and he was stronger than me because he wouldn't fight back. Someone said to me, 'You're not bad – he didn't hit you,' and now I got it. Why should I lower myself by fighting back? I knew if I hit back, then it would escalate to a whole different level, but if we talked, it would die down.

Sometimes I forget my past. My college friends don't know what I was into and I don't really get angry now. I go to church four times a week and I'm even a youth leader now. I pray a lot and read my Bible, particularly the story of David – he was a joker, but God loved him anyway. Some of the kids remind me of how I was and I talk to them about how I used to be. I try to guide them like Chris did to me – he didn't stop or give up on me, so I want to be positive to them. If they get angry, I try to stay calm and peaceful. I want to try my best to help them and it may be that even if they don't listen to me, I'm the first of a few people who will try and they'll get there in the end.

I'd really like to play football in the future. Chelsea scout us a lot. I used to think that I wouldn't want to be successful 'cos I preferred gang life to making money. If you became a millionaire you couldn't come back on the estate, you'd get robbed. Staying on the estate was more important to me. Now I see a couple of my friends playing for professional teams and think it could have been me if I'd not been so into the gang.

I also want to do youth work and help young kids in the situation I was in, to get them out. I hate all the statistics that say if you grow up in this area you're gonna grow up to be bad. I know that young people need role models. Someone like Boris Johnson doesn't mean anything to someone like me. All kids see are the older gang members who are in prison having loads of kids with different girls. You think, 'That's what I'll end up doing, so I might as well get used to it and do it now.' They need people who will talk to them one on one where they can be honest, not in a group where they all feed off each other. We also need things that get kids off the streets: if I'd had the opportunity to play football at night I'd have done that instead of going off robbing people.

I used to put on a front about the kind of person I was and eventually I started to believe it. Once you believe you're that person, you are that person. Now I'm a youth leader in my church and everyone loves me, even the ones who hated me before! My mum is smiling all the time and my sister is proud of me. I got a Christmas job and earned enough money to buy a laptop and it felt really good. I have positive friends now, none of them are violent and there aren't that many gangs in college. Last time someone called me up to fight, people were like, 'Elijah is peaceful – he don't fight!' and that felt good. I used to be a bit racist and thought white people were there to be robbed. Now my best friend is white and I hang around with an Indian guy too. Recently I came off the football pitch and my friend's little brother said to me, 'I want to be like you.' I almost cried that he said I was great. It made me so proud when I never used to have much to feel proud about.

3

Who Is Involved?

> At a certain age you just want to be accepted at certain
> levels. It's supposed to be like a family – at the end of the
> day it's all about acceptance and belonging to something
> because there ain't nothing else to belong to.
> (*Gang member, Birmingham*)[1]

To understand gangs we must understand the individuals
involved in them. How old are they? Where do they live?
What race and sex are they? Some of these factors are fairly
straightforward. For example, gangs tend to be found in deprived
inner-city neighbourhoods – London, Manchester, Birmingham,
Sheffield, Nottingham, Leeds and Bristol all have significant gang
problems. That said, gangs are by no means isolated to these cities,
but are beginning to spread into every part of England.[2]

ETHNICITY

It is easy to think of gangs as simply a problem for black communities, but while there are a disproportionate number of black males
in gangs, the stereotype does not tell the full story. Since gangs
tend to form among young people who live near each other, their
ethnic make-up tends to reflect the ethnicity of the population of

their area. In Glasgow and Salford, for example, gang members tend to be white, but in Brixton and Moss Side they are black. In areas like Sheffield, where a number of different ethnicities are represented, that is reflected in the fact that gangs have white, black and Asian members. So while membership of some gangs is based on ethnicity (such as Paki Panthers, Asian Virus and African Nations Crew, who identify their race in their names), most gangs are more concerned that members are from the same postcode than from the same racial background.

GANG MEMBERS ARE GETTING YOUNGER

For years most gangs have had a hierarchy of Elders (who are usually aged between eighteen and thirty) and Youngers (who are in their mid-teens). The Elders call the shots and the Youngers look up to the Elders and do their running for them. For example, an Elder may want to shoot someone without running the risk of being caught and facing a long prison sentence. If he asks a Younger to carry out the shooting on his behalf, he knows he will get the job done without risk to himself and the Younger can prove his commitment to the gang and impress his Elders.

If it was not frightening enough thinking of thirteen- and four-teen-year-olds being encouraged into criminal behaviour, it now seems there is a growing trend for Tinies to join gangs – children as young as seven and eight. Because of their age they are less likely to be stopped by the police, so they can run drugs money for the gang, earning cash for themselves in the process. There are rumours now of even younger children getting involved in gangs. They are known as Babies. Police officers tell me they know of gangs whose eldest members and leaders are fourteen-year-old boys. They all carry knives and their after-school activities tend to revolve around robberies. One north London police officer said, 'We see thirteen- and fourteen-year-old boys who have been stabbed four or five times. The blades go millimetres from their arteries, threatening their lives, but it doesn't shake them up. Instead they think they are invincible.'

Some of the boys involved in gangs are simply too young to grasp what they are doing. They just do not seem to understand that they could lose their lives and not even make it to the age of sixteen.

On the other hand, some teenage boys assume that they will not live to see many of their adult years, so they embrace the chaos and mayhem of gang lifestyle while they can, counting each day as a bonus. Greater Manchester Police have said that the average life expectancy of anyone involved in gun crime is just twenty-four years.[3]

OLDER BROTHERS

Although Elders call the shots in a gang, they are also likely to look after the Youngers and Tinies and protect them from any trouble. It is almost like a father or big brother role, where the Elders teach the younger ones, passing on what they know about making money and gaining respect. If a Younger or Tiny gets into any trouble, the person they turn to is their Elder. In the book *Street Boys*, Pod, who was involved in The 28s, a London-based gang, said, 'The 28s would protect the younger guys. The 28s were role models and we tried to be role models for each other. It's like fathering each other. Some of our parents couldn't parent us so if we tiefed [sic] a packet of crisps we would share it round. There was never a day that someone would be hungry.'[4]

In order to gain respect and achieve a reputation, Youngers and

Tinies are willing to risk everything. Since under-sixteens cannot go to prison, they can get away with a lot more, making them more likely to take chances and get involved in crazy things. They even see going to jail as something exciting, an aspiration. When Ribz (whose story is also told in *Street Boys*) was sixteen he finally went to prison after being involved in gangs and violence for years. He said that he was excited, that he'd always wanted to go to prison: 'It was kinda exciting for me still, the first time. I really wanted to go to jail. Everyone used to boast about it, innit? It was like a craze. I remember saying to myself, "I wanna go to jail, I wanna go to jail." So when I did go I was kinda excited . . . I was all like dancing and everything.'[5]

As well as feeling as if it is good for their reputations, jail can also provide useful contacts or links, as Joe said: 'Youngers actually want to go to jail now because that's where they'll make links; they'll meet other gang members. If they sleep in a cell with a guy who's been in there for a while then they'll be cool with each other and rolling with them when they get out. They come out of jail more powerful than they went in because of the link-ups.'

GIRLS IN GANGS

When you are as desperate as most of us are in that situation, you do anything to get what feels like love . . . The boys would treat us as their bitches, phone whoever they felt like f***ing, order them to come over, and most girls would drop everything and do whatever was wanted.
(*Laura, former gang member*)[6]

Although the vast majority of gang members are male (probably as high as 90–98 per cent), there are girls who get involved in gangs and the last few years have seen a few all-girl gangs emerge. Many girls are not active members, but are on the periphery of gangs and get used for a number of things, including:

- setting up rival gang members;
- as decoys;
- for sex;
- as handlers of drugs and weapons;
- to lure other girls;
- as lookouts;
- to increase a man's status.

The aim for most girls involved with gangs is to become the girlfriend of the gang leader, as that means she will be seen as someone in the community – it gives her status. He will usually look after her too, giving her drugs, buying her clothes and making sure she is protected from rape by other guys. But often there is little choice for the girl about whether she wants to be involved with a guy anyway: if he picks her, it is hard for her to say no and virtually impossible for her to break up with him.

Debbie, someone I met on my visits to Trenchtown, was called a Gun Girl because she used to look after the weapons for the men. She said, 'I wouldn't go out with a man unless he had a gun because if he didn't have a gun he wasn't a big man. I was desperate for love and was going to one man after another and the higher up they were in the gang, the better it was for my self-esteem.'

Because girls have traditionally attracted less suspicion than boys, gang members often give their weapons and drugs to the girls to look after. Members of the police told me that if they approach a group of young people on the street they will see the girls begin to shuffle away to start disposing of whatever they have on them. In one recent incident they said that they searched nearby bins after approaching a group and found a hammer, a can of mace and a couple of stolen wallets that the girls had dumped. Girls also seem to be getting involved in other criminal activities with gangs, helping out by dressing up as a man and luring rivals so that their own gang can ambush them. They are also taking a more active part in robberies, particularly on the streets. Females will approach a target and ask a question to distract them so that the guys can pounce and rob them.

This increase in criminal activity is matched by an increase in girls becoming more aggressive and violent and starting to fight alongside their male counterparts. The Youth Justice Board report a 25 per cent increase in offences committed by girls aged between ten and seventeen over the past three years – with a 50 per cent increase in violent offences. There has also been an increase in female gangs, often set up to impress the male gangs, and although only a handful are currently known about, they are just as serious in their violence as the guys. In 2009 two teenage girls were sent to prison for stripping a sixteen-year-old victim naked and whipping her with belts because the gang leader felt she had disrespected her mum. Another girl stood by and took photos of the attack on her mobile. One of the attackers said she wished she could have got guys there for the attack so she could have seen the victim raped.

Some of the girls in mixed gangs work hard to be 'one of the boys', dressing themselves as guys and acting as aggressively as their male counterparts. Many say that the girls are becoming even more savage than the guys in an attempt to prove themselves. As Laura said, 'I could be even tougher, more savage than [the boys] because I had to prove myself. I got into every level of violence – there was nothing a boy would do that I wouldn't match. I didn't care what I did: as I saw it, everyone judged me as bad, so I'd be bad. By doing that, I got what felt like respect, although I can see now how badly the boys treated me sometimes.'[7]

There have been a number of high-profile cases over the last few years where girls have been involved in savage attacks. Rosimeiri Boxall, a vicar's daughter, was killed trying to escape from a girl gang who were holding her hostage; and Sian Simpson was stabbed to death with a steak knife by another girl during a row over a man. There have been reports of sadistic attacks from girls too, such as the one on seventy-one-year-old Lily Lilley who was bound, had her false teeth pushed down her throat and was then thrown into a canal by two teenage girls. A girl gang is also suspected of making a liquid-based bomb that they threw into a girl's house, destroying it and two neighbouring houses. The row was about a boy.

Why are girls being drawn into such lifestyles? As Amy put it, 'The gangs I joined seemed the only people in the world to offer a kind of comfort and caring. The desire to feel wanted and included, in a world that seemed to regard me as scum, was very powerful.'

RAPE AS A WEAPON

One of the most common ways girls are used by gangs is for sex. Many of the guys do not have relationships, they have a series of 'links', meaning girls who will have sex with them without commitment. They phone a girl, ask her for sex and if she says yes, they ask if their 'brethren' can come and have sex with her too. This they refer to as a 'line-up', where one girl performs sexual acts with a group of men in turn. Their justification is that if the girl does not respect herself enough not to do it, why should they respect her?

What is even more horrifying than the way girls and sex are treated so incredibly casually is the fact that gangs also use rape as a weapon. Girls from rival gangs, as well as sisters and girlfriends of rival gang members, are all targets. In some cases initiation into a gang involves raping someone first. They will even rape a girl who belongs to their own gang if they believe she has betrayed them in some way.

Suzy, a young girl living in Hackney, was not involved in a gang, but a friend of hers, Angie, started hanging out with one. Suzy told Angie she did not think one of the guys in the gang was a very nice person and Angie reported that back to the guy in question. He rounded up three mates and together they waited for Suzy after school, grabbed her just a few feet from her own front door and threatened her with a knife. They took her to a nearby block of flats and then forced her to give them oral sex before one boy raped her. Her ordeal did not stop there. They rang more friends who came and joined the attack – nine of them in total, one as young as twelve, all assaulting one girl for the crime of one offensive remark.[8]

Some gangs deny responsibility for rape altogether, claiming that if a girl goes somewhere with a guy on her own, then it is her own fault if she gets raped. In Jo's case, she was just going over to a friend's house to play video games at his invitation. They had known each other since they were nine, had played together and hung out together, and she trusted him. But he had set a trap for her. When she arrived, two other guys were there and they raped her.

The girls do not even protect each other. Susan, who got involved with a gang at the age of thirteen, said she was involved in setting up a number of girls in order for them to be raped. The girls in question had slept with Susan's boyfriend, but her retaliation was to allow six or seven of the gang members to rape them. Another girl described how she would watch the gang she was involved in rape girls on a bus. The first time she said she was shocked and screamed at them to stop. By the second time she said her heart was hardened and she became emotionless, not caring about the other girls or anyone any more.

There is often a sense of powerlessness from many of the girls who get involved in this sort of thing, sometimes because they have gone through high levels of abuse in their own home. Amy, who was quoted earlier, was raped repeatedly by her stepfather from the age of four years old. She used drugs to escape the pain of her abuse from as young as six and began getting involved with male gang members from just twelve.

If girls do get raped or forced to have sex with more than one gang member, it will usually go unreported. Cases are hard to prove and the girls may still want to hang out with the gang as it is the equivalent of their family. One of the main reasons, though, is that there is little trust in the police and most girls do not even consider reporting the crime to be an option, having been brought up around people who called the police 'the enemy'. The main reason is that there is a huge fear of reprisal – no one wants to snitch on a gang for fear of what they will do to them in return. One girl said she walked into a room at a party and saw a gang rape taking place. She could hear the girl crying, saw that her tights had been ripped and that she was bleeding, but she was too scared to do anything in case they came after her next. She closed the door and walked away. The fear the gangs generate means they know they can get away with anything and so they often do not even try to hide their identity. Some even film their attacks and then boast about them, showing the footage around school or to their mates.

It is incredibly shocking to hear about girls caught up in such violence and crime. Some are the innocent victims left scarred by such horrific attacks. Others are actively embracing the lifestyle of gangs for themselves. What is clear is that joining a gang is becoming increasingly popular for both sexes and for kids so young that they should not have a care in the world. The real question we need to look at is why it has become so appealing.

DEZ'S STORY

I learned to look after myself pretty early on in life. My mum is white and my dad black and when I was growing up in the late 1970s/early 1980s that was still quite unusual, so we stood out as a family. I was one of only four black people at my secondary school and was more than aware of the racial tension in my borough. There were areas I knew to avoid or I'd increase the chances of getting attacked for my colour and I remember being chased by about fifty National Front guys one time shouting 'Get them niggers!' There were only a few of us so there wasn't much we could do except run.

When I was about thirteen I started drinking alcohol; I took an old Orangina bottle and filled it with a concoction of spirits from home. My mates and I loved the thrill of getting drunk and even started drinking in lessons, hiding our cans of Tennent's from the teachers. I enjoyed school, though, and never got kicked out. I knew how to wear a mask and hide anything I was doing wrong. My older brother and I were quite enterprising so we made a bit of money by selling videos we'd got from a local shop to other pupils.

I started hanging around with guys who were older than me and they used to use hash and weed. I tried it and liked it, so then I took LSD too, just to see what it was like. The experimental use became social use and soon I was psychologically addicted as it formed part of my lifestyle. Friends were taking speed and cocaine, so I did too and by the age of sixteen I was selling drugs too. The drugs totally changed my mood, making me quite narrow minded and selfish. I'd take cocaine, often mixing it up with hash which would make me feel heavy, then the cocaine would give me a high. I started getting involved in street robberies. It wasn't like I needed the money – I just chose to rob people because I was a wannabe. I was working on a market stall and earning a fair wage, but I took extra cash from the stall when I could. Eventually they had to let me go because they weren't making enough money so my own stealing did me out of a job. Because I'd been getting away with these things I got greedy. The greedier you get, the bigger risks you take. You stop planning your robberies and your drug selling and just start stealing and dealing to anyone, which of course increases the chance that you'll get caught, but you don't care.

I carried a knife which I used for the street robberies; most of the time when you threatened someone with it they gave you what you wanted pretty quickly. One time a guy wouldn't back down. I wanted his ring and he wouldn't give it to me. It felt like he was disrespecting me, that he wasn't scared of me and didn't believe that I would use the knife. I felt like I had no option so I stabbed him several times in his leg. I felt a real rush of adrenalin after the knife went in; I felt so in control. Of course sometimes we came off worse in fights; my brother almost lost his eye after a particularly nasty incident. Five of us had gone into someone else's territory and were being loud and drawing attention to ourselves; the girls were starting to notice us. The guys there didn't like it – there were about thirty of them so we didn't stand a chance. The repercussion of this stand-off was several weeks later when my brother got cut right across his face and had to have twenty-nine stitches. Thankfully his eye was OK, but it was a sign of how serious things were getting. Even my mum, dad, aunt and uncle got involved, planning how to get back at the boy who had slashed my brother's face, talking about shooting or knee-capping him. We'd always been able to talk to our parents about what was going on and the discussions became more graphic as we found ourselves in difficult situations. It's shocking how these things affect and can influence even the most balanced minds; one time I shared with my mum about an incident I was involved in and she recommended I stab the person in the arm in defence and not the stomach as it's less likely to cause major problems/harm. My previously law-abiding and moral parents were being drawn into our world.

A few weeks later, my friends came round and said they wanted to go to a rave. It was acid music and I wasn't really into it, but they said they'd pay for me so I thought I'd go. We needed to get the ticket from a friend who was working in a shop and we had to walk through a park to get there. As we went through, my friend and a stranger in his early twenties caught each other's eye and began glaring at one another until there was a stand-off. They were screaming at each other and the guy started battering my friend. As I got closer he started swearing at me and my pride just wouldn't let me take that. I should have walked away, but instead I got in his face saying, 'Don't talk to me like that.' He swung for me and as I ducked I stabbed him in the stomach. This had stopped him in his tracks and I slowly started walking away, not wanting to draw attention to myself, but a couple heard the guy screaming and asked me if I'd hurt him. They realised he was pointing towards me and swung at me, but I ducked again and ran for it with his little dog chasing me. I ran all the way home and went straight upstairs to wash the knife. I tried not to think about what I'd done. I didn't feel remorseful; I thought he deserved it 'cos he shouldn't have confronted me. Anyway, I figured he couldn't be that badly injured as I'd only stabbed him once – maybe he'd need stitches, but I couldn't see it being that bad. Over the next twenty-four hours I told my mum and dad what had happened. My mum was a bit upset, but seemed to accept that this was how our lives were. My dad asked me to give him the knife and said he'd speak to me about it later.

Later that day, when I heard that the guy I'd stabbed was in intensive care, I wasn't really that bothered. It sounded kind of serious, but didn't mean that much to me so I carried on as normal. The next day, I was sat talking on the phone while my brother was watching *EastEnders* when there was a knock at the door. My brother answered and I could hear someone saying, 'He's killed him! He's killed him!' and the next thing I knew a group had pushed their way into the house and were attacking my brother. There were about fifteen of them, ranging from late teens to their thirties, and many of them had big reps in the area for the crazy stuff they'd done. They were so angry and they threw me down the stairs and started laying into me. They were stomping on both me and my brother 'til we were covered in cuts and bruises and there was no skin left on my back. The only reason they stopped was because a woman from over the road saw what was happening and ran over yelling at them. She was terrified they were going to kill us.

When they left, my brother and I instinctively grabbed

knives from the kitchen drawer and thought about going to the pub after them. Thankfully we realised it was a pretty bad idea and called mum and dad to inform them of what had happened. It wasn't long before they came home and then the police turned up. It only hit me that the guy was actually dead when the police said they were arresting me on suspicion of murder. I didn't really know what it meant in terms of what would happen to me, but I knew I just had to firm up and get on with it. My mum and dad stood there crying in shock as the police took me away. First I was taken to the hospital to have my injuries looked at. I had four officers with me and was handcuffed to one of them – they wouldn't uncuff me even while the doctors looked at me. Then I was taken to the police station where I stayed for the next two days. After going to court I was remanded in Brixton Prison. As I walked in, a guy called me over to his cell as I passed. 'What you in for?' he asked. 'Murder,' I replied and he put his fist through the pigeonhole and said, 'Respect.' It was a strange new reality to know the majority of society would be horrified at what I'd done, but here I was accepted.

The cell I was taken to was small, cold and had two buckets instead of a sink and toilet. As it started to dawn on me that I might be facing years in prison, I tried not to meditate on the negatives and knew that instead I had to adapt quickly to the new environment. I hardened my mind and told myself it couldn't last for ever. I wouldn't shower as I'd heard stories of what happened to young guys who did. I was skinny as a rake, but I knew I had to project a certain image in order to survive, so I would walk around projecting confidence and carry myself with the same attitude I'd used when on the road. It was a balance, though, as I didn't want to present myself as too hype as that would make me a target for trouble. The only reassuring thing was when I saw lots of familiar faces from the streets in there. But the seriousness of my crime set me apart from most of the others and meant the officers kept a close eye on me. Lots of family members came to see me, even ones I hadn't seen in years. They talked about getting me out of the country if I was ever released on bail, maybe sending me to stay with my sister in Jamaica. It seemed like it could be my best option if I didn't want to spend the rest of my life in a cell.

Within a week in prison my big mouth had already got me into a fight. I couldn't back down from a confrontation or I'd become an easy target and my cellmate's cousin made it known he had a problem with me. He was threatened by my friendship with my cellmate and we ended up in a fight in the shower block. He punched me in the face and my nose was bleeding. I was about to kick him in the head when someone told us the screws were coming. We broke it up, but after that we'd always be cussing one another through the cell windows whenever the opportunity arose.

My girlfriend came to visit me and said she'd been saved. 'Saved from what?' I asked. She told me she'd become a Christian, but I just wasn't interested. I believed there was a God, but had no understanding of any religion because it wasn't the way I'd been brought up. My god was my conscience and I justified my behaviour to myself, telling myself that I'd never intended to kill anyone and the guy I'd stabbed had deserved it. I didn't think I wanted or needed the God my girlfriend was talking about. My sister was a Christian too and she had been telling me to pray and read the Bible and so somehow I managed to get hold of one. I started a routine where each night I'd have a cigarette, do my weights and say a prayer before I went to bed. I'd pray for my family and friends and for myself. It sort of felt like counselling to me, being able to talk to God like that.

When I went to court the magistrate set the bail at £25,000 so my mum and dad had to sign their house over in case I did a runner. That put an end to the plans to send me to Jamaica. I came out having only spent four weeks in prison, but awaiting trial to see how long my sentence would be. The case had made the national press because the man I'd stabbed had been a soldier and his dad was quite high up in the police. My parents had to move house because of the hostility in the community, my friends would get bricks thrown through their windows and we received verbal death threats. Twice a day I had to sign in at a police station to prove I hadn't absconded, but my attitude hadn't changed. I still wasn't taking responsibility for what I'd done. I was still taking drugs, still going to areas I shouldn't be going to. I was in denial about my lifestyle and what the court case could mean for me. In the kind of culture I was in, a criminal record for something so serious was actually something that gave me kudos. I played on it like everyone else did and enjoyed the respect it granted me.

Before long I got into a fight with a guy over my girlfriend. We were on the fourth floor of his tower block and he brought two of his mates down, so we agreed to go down to the street to fight. I picked up a knife, but decided I didn't need it. We agreed not to use weapons and started fighting, but then he stabbed me twice in the leg. I went ballistic because we'd said we wouldn't use anything – so much for the 'code of the street'. I called a cab to take me to the hospital and tried to hide the fact I was bleeding. The cabbie wasn't happy when he saw there was blood all over the seat. I had to get stitches, which made me late to go and sign in at the police station, breaking my conditions of bail. I told them my train had been delayed and thankfully, because I'd always been on time before, they were lenient with me and let me off. When I got home my mum, dad and brother were all crying about what had happened, telling me I was destroying everything. For the first time it made me realise how selfish my attitudes and actions really were. I knew I was hurting the people I loved. I began to reflect on what my life had become.

My girlfriend asked me to go to church with her so I went along reluctantly. I had stopped praying since I'd left prison and hadn't really thought about God unless she mentioned him. But I went to church with an open heart and mind. It was a really traditional church with everyone dressed up in suits, and I was wearing shorts, with twists in my hair, so I really stood out. At the end of the service the pastor said that if anyone wanted forgiveness they should come to the front. Despite the ways I had justified it to myself, I knew I needed to be forgiven for taking someone's life, so I went forward, not really sure what would happen. They prayed for me and I felt overwhelmed, like I wasn't in control. I didn't like it, so I left, but I came back the next week. I was pretty bored during the service; I just wanted an emotional fix like I'd had before, so I left early and didn't go back for a few weeks. When I did go back the pastor made the same call – for anyone who wanted to be forgiven to go forward – so I went again. A woman started jumping up and down in front of me, crying with happiness and saying she'd been praying for me. I was struck by the love and passion in her actions. It made me think I wanted to get to know this God if he reacted to me the way this woman had.

All I'd been thinking about up until that point was how I could get back at the guy who stabbed me. I wanted revenge, but I started to wonder about where my life was going. Because of the things I'd done I was always looking over my shoulder, wondering who might be after me. I started to question if that was really what I wanted my life to be. I was really surprised that some of the people in church had similar backgrounds to me – they'd been involved in armed robberies, taken drugs, one had even been involved in a kidnapping. They were so passionate about what God had done in their lives and what he could do in mine that I started to think maybe I could get involved in church and God. They accepted me, which was something I'd never expected. They told me God was real, that he was able to do miracles and I just needed to believe. All my life the only person I had believed in was myself.

Over the next few weeks I really started to realise I needed help to change my attitude. I knew my life was out of control and I figured that if God could help me, I'd give him a try. I'd repented over the person I'd killed, but I began to realise there was so much more than that wrong in my life. My values system all got turned on its head. I'd never cared if it was wrong to take drugs, sleep around, carry a knife – even steal from someone if I thought they had enough money. I didn't even really value my own life. My new faith made me question all of that. I told my mum I believed in God and she asked me how I could when I looked at my life. When she started to see me change, though, she was so relieved that I wasn't getting into trouble any more that she accepted my beliefs.

In the midst of all this I was awaiting my court day. When I finally stood there as they read out my verdict, I held my breath. If they found me guilty of murder I could be looking at a life sentence. They said I was not guilty of murder, but of manslaughter, and gave me two years' probation. It was an incredibly lenient sentence and the prosecution appealed against it. Five months later I was back in court and this time I was sentenced to two years in custody. I went back to Brixton Prison and had to really keep myself from going back to my old ways. I was so tempted to take drugs and because of my reputation there was always someone looking to cause trouble with me. I wouldn't take the bait, though, and didn't get into any more fights or even cuss people. After a while people began to see that my faith was genuine and they respected me for that.

I've never spoken to the family of the guy I killed. I asked the police if they would let them know that I wanted to talk to them, but understandably they said no. I wanted to apologise for all the pain that I'd caused them. Although I'd changed and turned my life around, it couldn't bring back their son and they weren't convinced my conversion was genuine. The family wrote an article in the *Evening Standard* where the mum said that she hated me and the dad that he treated me with contempt.

I can't do anything to take back my actions, but the next best thing for me was to set up a project to stop other young people doing the things I had done. I've got four children of my own and I never want any of them to get involved in drugs, crime, knives or guns. I've set up a project that started in partnership with the police in Wandsworth, called Spark2Life, that works with youths who are at risk and tries to help them make positive lifestyle choices. The idea is that it is a preventative approach to changing behaviour, working with young people while they are in school, Pupil Referral Units, prison or with Youth Offending Teams. I use what I have experienced and learned to challenge their perceptions of crime. The programme is linked to the curriculum and has already seen a reduction in youth crime when working in partnership with the police in Wandsworth. I've worked directly with lots of young people on the brink of serious offences, like Kieron who, at the age of fifteen, was stabbed in a gang-related incident. He was intent on revenge, but after we spent time talking through the consequences of what he wanted to do he changed his mindset completely. He began to hang out with a totally new crowd, moved away from his old gang friendships, and as a result his behaviour has improved dramatically both at home and at school.

I'm very fortunate to have the opportunity to share my experience so I can try and impact a younger generation and help them make positive changes. If there's one thing I know, it's that we can't change our past but we can choose our future.

* * *

To read Dez's story in full, see *Convicted or Condemned* by Dez Brown and Martin Saunders, (Authentic Media, 2005).

Part Two

What Drives People Into Gangs?

Before we look at the things that drive young people towards gangs, we need to be clear that it is rarely just one of these factors working in isolation that will steer an individual down that path. From the stories in this book you will see that there is usually a combination of problems at play. It is unlikely that just because a young person has a difficult home life they will turn to a gang. If they struggle in school, they may truant or misbehave, but again it will not automatically push them towards a gang. A child can grow up in poverty and not see drug dealing or robbery as the answer. That said, all these factors play a part and when they are combined they can have a powerful and sometimes overwhelming effect on a young person. Over the next few chapters we will look at these factors and try to address some of the issues surrounding them, so that we can get a holistic picture of what many of our young people are facing and what makes joining a gang seem appealing.

4

Family

At the heart and soul of it is the breakdown of the family . . . It is not fashionable to say, but absolutely, unequivocally, any attempt to address these issues without addressing the breakdown of the family will only have limited impact.

(*Superintendent John Sutherland, Islington Borough Police*)

We have long been aware of the breakdown of the traditional family unit. Now one child in four is brought up by a single parent. In 90 per cent of those cases, it is the mother who is raising the children, leaving a huge lack of father figures in homes across the country. High rates of divorce are of course a major contributing factor, as well as people having babies when they are not married or living together, and the tragic death of one parent. Through working on estates I have realised that it is not uncommon for young people to say they do not even know how many stepbrothers and sisters they have because their mum has had children with lots of different partners. In these situations there may be a man living with them, but he is not their father and often these temporary father figures do not stay long. They have been referred to as 'guesting fathers' and it only adds to the insecurity in a child's life when a number of men come and go, trying to take on the role of their father for a short time.

It seems to be the case that a disruptive home life can result in children looking to gangs rather than their parents for security. However, there are many one-parent families across the country whose children never go near a gang or get into trouble. Of course there are countless valid reasons why many women or men are looking after their children alone. Despite this, though, the statistics regarding children brought up by a lone parent are frightening. Children of lone parents are:

- 75 per cent more likely to fail in school;
- 70 per cent more likely to be drug addicts;
- 50 per cent more likely to have an alcohol problem;
- 35 per cent more likely to experience unemployment/welfare dependency.[1]

It is also true that children exposed to violence in the home are more likely to become violent themselves. The Street Weapons Commission cites that 40 per cent of boys and young men and 25 per cent of girls and young women in custody have experienced violence at home. I have seen this in many of the young people I have come into contact with, who grow up surrounded by adults who sort their problems out using their fists. This becomes the norm to them. In addition, 63 per cent of boys who are brought up by fathers who have been convicted of a crime go on to be convicted themselves.[2] Again, they are a product of their upbringing and what has been represented to them as acceptable behaviour.

It is helpful to say upfront that when you look at issues around families whose children have turned to violence there are some stereotypical images of parents who do not care, leaving their kids alone, letting them do what they like. Although it would be naive to think that does not happen, it is also important to note that there are plenty of parents who are desperate to keep their kids out of gangs and away from trouble, but find themselves powerless to do so. Many impress upon their children the importance of doing well at school, keeping their noses clean and staying out of trouble. At the same time they are aware that if their children do not know how to handle themselves, they can, and most likely will, find themselves in danger. The parents therefore feel forced to equip their kids with the ability to handle themselves just so that they can survive in their neighbourhood.

A PLACE TO BELONG

One of the key issues in deprived areas is that single parents (usually mothers) are forced to work long hours, sometimes in multiple jobs, in order to support themselves and their family. Their motives may be purely to provide and get by, but their absence can mean that their children are left to fend for themselves for a large proportion of the time. It is not unusual (particularly on estates) for even very young children to be left to wander around after school. We have had four-year-olds come into our youth projects on estates, completely on their own and without any supervision or anyone knowing where they are. So many young kids are left with no one to cook for them or to help them with their homework; often the older ones are left in charge of their younger siblings even if they themselves are under ten.

In an ideal world, a family is a safe place, a haven from the rest of the world, somewhere you feel known, cared for and understood. With so many young people not seeing even one parent from one day to the next, they have no stable family unit and are left feeling they have no place where they belong. For lots of young people a gang becomes a lifeline which plugs the gap left by their absent parents, and almost 60 per cent of young people say that finding a sense of identity is a key reason to join a gang.[3] Gangs are often described as being like family units where 'brothers' look after 'brothers' and friends call each other 'cuz' (for cousin) even though they are not related by blood.

Phat Si said he started to take his gang (the PDC or the Peel Dem Crew) seriously when he realised what the friendships within it meant to him: 'With JaJa, Inch and a couple of other brudders, I've never had an incident where I've had an argument with them. We've never come to blows. All my life I've noticed there's not a lot of people I'm like that with. I've come to blows all the time. Bare blows. But never with these guys. I saw the love from them. I trust my brudders. That's the time really and truly when I took PDC serious.'[4]

Until he was eight years old, Si's life was great. With five sisters and parents who adored him, he was happy, safe and secure. But that all changed out of the blue when one day he came home to find his mother had left the country, taking his sisters with her. There was no warning and no explanation. His dad said he could not cope bringing Si up alone and so he was sent to live with his elderly grandma who could not keep a very close eye on him. Can you even imagine what that must be like for an eight-year-old child? Being left by his mother and losing his sisters all in one day, then being sent away from his dad to live with an old woman? Si turned to his friends and to a gang which led him to get shot, stabbed, arrested, beaten up and ultimately almost took his life. He went to a club one night with other PDC members looking to buy drugs. A fight broke out, gunshots followed and one hit Si in the head. Lucky to be alive, Si was paralysed down one side, leaving many years of rehab ahead of him if he ever hoped to walk and talk. Before the shooting Si said, 'Eight years old. That's when my life went downhill. From eight years old no one looked after me. I just lived on the streets and made do by myself. There was no one except me and my friends.'[5]

This part of Si's story is not unusual. Many children find their life turned upside down when one parent leaves and, with no steady home life, young people look elsewhere for their needs to be met. Gangs, in contrast, seem to offer a place to belong, a group of people who have got your back no matter what goes on, a sense of loyalty and even unconditional love. As Si said, his friends were there for him in a way that his family was not.

John Sutherland of Islington Borough Police told me how, after one particular London gang murder, they found that of the thirteen young people initially suspected of involvement in the killing, twelve were from lone-parent homes and one was living with step-parents. That is just one of the examples that has led him to believe that family is at the heart of our growing gang problem.

A FATHERLESS GENERATION

As I said earlier, the situation in places like Jamaica is a lot more advanced than it is in the UK, giving us an ominous idea of what the future could hold for our country if we do not address the problems now. I shall never forget standing in a school in Trenchtown, in front of a few hundred kids, knowing that 90 per cent of them had no dad around. Ninety per cent! Unlike here, where family breakdown is the most common cause of absent fathers, in Jamaica the violence has escalated to the point where most kids have lost their fathers to gun crime. What will life be like for this almost fatherless generation?

For the women in Trenchtown there is great fear. Not only have so many lost their partners, but they are absolutely terrified of losing their children too, as the cycle of violence continues. One mum took me to the exact spot where she had lost her son just a few weeks before I arrived. She was very tearful and when I asked how I could pray for her, she said, 'Pray that the war will stop.'

One woman I have come to know through my trips to Trenchtown with the XLP team is Debbie, a local assistant head-teacher who was a Gun Girl for many years until her brother was killed in a drive-by shooting. On my most recent trip, Debbie's son showed me a wound right by his spine where he had been hit by a stray bullet. The doctors left the bullet where it was as it was too close to his spine to remove it safely. Debbie said she had begged him not to go the same way as his father, who was killed through gang violence. I have met many parents here in the UK who are desperate to keep their children away from gangs. Some have told me they struggle to sleep at night for worrying about what their kids might be getting up to. Others have tried to move out of the inner city to places where they perceive their kids will not be tempted by the gang lifestyle. Other parents try not to let their kids go out at all, and as a result are forced to stay at home themselves to keep an eye on them. One parent we have been working with at XLP now goes out only when they know their child is out with an XLP coach.

It is not as simple as telling the parents they need to do a better job. Their kids are living in an environment where they see violence all around them and they become numb to it. It starts to become the norm, 'just the way things are', and the way they see their own lives heading because they cannot see any way out of it.

One person who was interviewed for *Dying to Belong* commented, 'Telling these families to take responsibility for their kids' behaviour is like telling them to take their kids into the jungle and take responsibility for them not getting eaten by lions and tigers.'[6]

Another common factor is that, with no father figure around, young guys feel they have to step into the role of being the 'man of the house' and sort out matters such as finances for the family. They desperately want to look after their mums and feel a sense of duty to bring in money to support them. So, when gangs offer a good amount of money for selling drugs and stolen goods, the temptation is great. These young men are growing up under pressure to take on a father figure role, even though they are still children themselves.

Similarly, girls can often be forced to take on the role of 'mother' in the home while their mum is working multiple jobs to keep the family going. They take care of younger siblings, getting them dressed, fed and ready for school. They do the food shopping and the washing as their parents are not around to do these things for them. Often, these very young children are facing the kinds of responsibilities most of us do not come across until after we have left home. They are forced to make adult decisions when they are too young to understand the consequences fully.

TEENAGE PARENTS

You might know that the UK has the highest teen pregnancy rate in all of Western Europe and the second highest rate in the world.[7] Most teenage pregnancies involve the poorest girls in the poorest parts of the country and many teenage mums were themselves born to young girls.[8] Again, this has a huge impact on the stability of family life. How can a fourteen-year-old single mum instil good values in her son or daughter when she herself is still struggling to learn who she is and what she believes? Boys who are fathering children at such a young age are having kids with a number of different women, to the extent that some children are growing up having no idea who their half-brothers and sisters are. This was the case for Ribz, who found out while visiting his mum in prison that the boy and girl sitting across the room from him were actually his half-brother and sister whom he had never met or even known about. His mother said that his dad had fathered children with a few different women from their area, but his dad was not even around for him to be able to find out who they were. From then on, if Ribz saw a girl he liked on the estate, he was terrified of chatting her up in case it turned out they had the same father.

THE HARDEST JOB IN THE WORLD

Everyone knows that children do not come with a handbook and parenting is the hardest job in the world. I am lucky enough to be the father of three amazing kids, but I feel as if I am making it up as I go along. Before my wife Diane and I became parents, the only thing we were taught was how to breathe in labour and, to be honest, that went out of the window after the first contraction. We all tend to parent our kids similarly to the way we were brought up. Our parents are our role models and, consciously or not, we tend to repeat history. What does that mean if you have never had a dad yourself? How do you learn how to father? How do you create a safe and loving home when you have never had one yourself? I shall always remember a fourteen-year-old girl I met at one school telling me that her greatest ambition was to be a single mum because she 'didn't want no man getting in the way and messing things up'. That was her answer to the way she had seen her dad treat her mum – she would rather do it on her own.

Over recent years, many community organisations and churches have begun parenting courses for the local community to help address some of the issues. These can be fantastic, but the real key is for us all to be in it together. We must recognise that when it comes to bringing up kids, we are all trying to work it out and even the best parents make mistakes.

Leroy grew up on a large estate in south-west London which is lined with tower blocks and is rife with drugs. Leroy's whole life changed at the age of nine when his father died. Having internalised his feelings, Leroy grew increasingly angry. The lack of support he received at school for his dyslexia made him feel even more furious and he took it out on his teachers, leading to his expulsion during his GCSE year. With things getting harder at home, Leroy found himself kicked out at the age of sixteen, so he moved in with a friend and got involved with life on the streets. His friendship group developed into a gang, which he says gave him the family he did not have at home. The gang fought other areas, committed street robberies and sold drugs for money, wanting to get their name out there and gain respect. Before he was seventeen, Leroy had been stabbed twice, once in the face when being robbed while selling drugs and once when a fight broke out because he and his friends were in another gang's territory. The second stabbing was in the leg, narrowly missing an artery. It was then that he realised this was no family – when his 'friends' left him bleeding on the street.

In many cases gangs do act like brothers, taking the rap for each other and keeping each other's backs. In other cases, as Leroy found out, everyone is looking out for themselves and will run to keep themselves out of trouble. As Elijah pointed out earlier, some gangs have become more volatile now, with the Youngers looking to prove themselves and so turning on their Elders. This means that gangs cultivate an atmosphere of fear as much as affection.

Leroy said, 'No one wants to be in a gang, it's the only choice they've got.'[9]

JANE'S STORY

I've been working in a prison for eight years and over that time I've seen a huge increase in the numbers of young people coming in who have been involved in gangs, many of whom are on trial for murder or manslaughter. Some of these young people are entrenched in gang life as they've been involved since they were as young as eleven. Lots of them wouldn't classify themselves as being in a gang: to them it's just the friends they've grown up with and they see each other as family. Their language reflects this, as they call each other 'fam' for short, 'blood' for blood brother, or 'bred' for brethren, and they often refer to someone who isn't related to them as 'cuz' for cousin. To them their friends are their family and they will do all they can to look out for each other.

For the last six years I have been the prison chaplain and although a lot of the young people are in for violent crimes, when I meet them I don't see a hardened criminal, I see a child who is crying out to be loved. Lots of the young men are dealing with huge issues of rejection. Many are from single-parent families, often with little or no contact with their fathers. Some have been sent away by their parents (who live abroad) to stay with aunts and uncles over here. Often they grow up without boundaries and become like children gone wild. Anyone who has been around a young child knows they are naturally naughty and have tantrums and need to be shown what is acceptable by someone who loves them. If a toddler isn't taught to behave through a combination of love, praise and boundaries, they can become out of control and never learn to stop acting like toddlers. For many of the people I work with, this is the case. They act like toddlers with muscles, knives and guns. Many of them may want the lifestyle that goes with gang activity, like a flash car and jewellery, but for the most part it seems to me they just want to feel special and important – they want a place to belong.

With the absence of fathers in their own lives, boys often struggle when they become parents themselves, because they haven't got a clue what it means to be a good dad. Sadly, many of them become fathers while they are still pretty much children themselves. A lot of the young men come to see me when their girlfriends have given birth and we arrange baby visits. One of the main jobs we need to do is to re-educate them about the best way to provide for their family. They often think about the material things that were lacking in their own lives growing up and are determined to provide better for their children. Some turn to crime to get money so they can buy their families things like designer clothes, but what we try to show them is that love is worth far more than anything they can buy. If they weren't loved as a child themselves, it's hard for them to get their heads around the fact that their children are better off with fewer material things and a father who cares and is around to bring them up.

Nearly every day I see at least one young man in tears. They are often worried about their mums, girlfriends and the families left behind. Interestingly, they do not usually cry tears of remorse for their crime or their victims. That doesn't mean they are heartless, but because they are teenagers they often struggle to see beyond their own little world. Though this is common for teenagers of all backgrounds, what makes these young men so different is that they feel that no one cares about them. In many ways they can't face up to what they've done, because if they start to think about the impact of their actions on someone else, they also have to face the impact of other people's actions against them. They live in a world where they have to justify why their dad never sees them, or why he beat them or their mum. 'I was unlucky' is the only way they can make sense of it and so they justify their own actions with the idea that the person they stole from or hurt was just unlucky too. One of the keys to stopping criminals from reoffending is to help them look at their victims and really see the impact of their crimes. For those who are willing, we help them through a programme such as the Sycamore Project run by Prison Fellowship. It is a six-session course where a group explores the effects of crime on victims, offenders and the community and discusses what it means to take responsibility for their actions. During one of the sessions a victim of crime visits to talk about how it has impacted their lives. Being able to show empathy for their victims is part of a process that comes with time. I've seen people completely change through doing the Sycamore Project, even to the point where they have changed their plea because they don't want to put their victim through the pain of being on the stand in court.

Prison can improve the young people who come in. Some find that with everything stripped away from them, they come face to face with what they have done and what they want their life to be. Some really flourish in prison, because they actually feel cared for and some of the work they do gives them a sense of achievement. Whenever we run some kind of course such as the Sycamore Project or the Labyrinth (an interactive prayer walk), they always ask for a certificate. It may be just a piece of paper, but it means so much to them as it shows they've achieved something. For many, if they don't have support when they leave, they just go back to what they know once they're out of prison, even if they were initially determined to stay out of trouble. Others make more connections and links while inside and go on to commit further crimes as a result. We even have some who feel safer in prison than out, because there the gangs can't get to them.

Prison isn't quite how the media often portray it. Some make it look like a holiday camp, others talk about it as though it's incredibly violent and out of control. Prisoners have a basic standard of living and if they work hard they can receive extra privileges. They take part in education and workshops and, although they may have a TV in their room, at the end of the day someone else gets to say when they can leave that room, so it's definitely not a bed of roses.

I spend a lot of my time working one to one with people who are finding it difficult to cope. They just need someone to listen without judging them. Often no one's actually listened to them or cared about them before. I never ask what they've done to get into prison. Some want to tell me to get it off their chest; others say they were innocent and feel they've been stitched up. Regardless of their circumstances, I am there to talk to them about how to get through the situation in front of them. When I ask one of the young people, 'What do you really want?' they tell me they just want to have a normal life. They just want to have a job, a wife, a house, but to them that sounds as much a fantasy as you or I saying we want to be a film star: they may dream about it, but they can't see it ever actually happening.

5

Role Models

I know that young people need role models . . . All kids see are the older gang members who are in prison having loads of kids with different girls. You think, 'That's what I'll end up doing, so I might as well get used to it and do it now.'

(*Elijah, ex-gang member*)

One of the clear problems for boys growing up without fathers is a real lack of positive role models. A Prince's Trust report found that more than a third of those aged between sixteen and twenty-five say they do not have a parent they consider a role model and so look to their peer group instead.[1] Young people will always seek someone to look up to, and more often than not young children idolise their dads. If he is absent either physically or emotionally, they will look for the nearest man to demonstrate what manhood is. The trouble on an estate is that sometimes the man they are likely to look to is a gang leader. He seems to have it all together, he is well known, everyone respects him, no one messes with him, he has a serious amount of money, he has girls and he drives a nice car. He probably also has a criminal record, a number of guns and a drug business. But this is the person the young guys are looking to when they are trying to find out what it means to be a man. He is the one they want to get in with so that they have someone looking after them; he is the one they are loyal to for taking care of them.

One of the things I have learned from visiting people who work with gangs in other countries is that we can save ourselves a lot of pain in the future if we are willing to work with young people now. Instead of demonising them for their actions, we need to find ways to help them change. Through my work with XLP I have visited places like Jamaica and Ghana to understand more about black history and gang culture. Recently I returned to Trenchtown in Jamaica, hoping for signs of change from my first visit and longing to catch up with some of the people I had met who were working hard to get out of gangs. Sadly, things had changed for the worse. We had barely touched down when we heard the devastating news that Pastor David was dead. He was a well-respected man in the community. I had met him on a previous visit and had been blown away by all that he was doing to help gang members get out of their situations. One of the gang members, Destruction, would always tell me how influential Pastor David was among the gangs and their families. He would often visit people at home, helping them find employment opportunities and doing mediation work between the gangs. No one ever had a bad word to say about him. They only ever praised him for the fact that his spirituality was more than just words – he was involved in very practical ways. Just before we arrived, he had been found dead in his own home with his throat cut. Along with the vast majority of the community, we were shocked. We were told this news on the way from the airport and, as we drove through Trenchtown, we could not help but notice that the streets were quiet; people were staying inside because of the fear that this violent act on an innocent man had brought. Even in Trenchtown, which is known for its violence, this was an unusual killing. People are frequently shot on the streets, but rarely killed in their own homes.

That evening there was a thanksgiving service for Pastor David. Sadly, many who wanted to pay their respects were forced to stay at home as the church was outside their block and therefore unsafe for them to travel to. Although it was a devastating loss to the community, the service was incredible. Despite their pain, people were praising God passionately and when I spoke to some of them after the service, I found their stories were tragic. Many told me that in some parts of the country, if someone wants revenge, they will not shoot you, they will kill one of your children instead. One woman they knew had recently been killed when her house was torched. She was found dead in the shower, her arms wrapped around her seven-year-old daughter. Another ex-gang leader told me of a time when a gang had torched a house with children inside. Their mother had tried to run in to rescue them, but the gang fired shots across the house to stop anyone from getting inside. I found these stories really hard to take – such a waste of life and the victims were completely innocent.

I also met a guy called Terrance whose street name was Bleach. He told me he joined a gang at the age of nine. As a little kid he would stay up all night watching what the gangs were getting up to, desperate to join in. He wanted to be like the older gang members with their money, their girls, their designer labels. Bleach said his dad was not around, his mum was always at work and the gang lifestyle seemed exciting – until his best friend was killed when he was seventeen. Now he is doing all he can to be a positive influence in the community, working with other ex-gang members to help young guys and girls respect themselves and stay away from gangs.

During my time in Trenchtown I met a woman called Miss Lorna, who works with gang members in the area. Born in Panama, Lorna arrived in Jamaica aged eight and now, in her fifties, she heads up Operation Restoration, a fantastic project seeking to serve communities in and around Trenchtown. Over the last ten years she has set up many programmes covering after-school clubs, outreach into local communities, a 'Youth Off the Streets' initiative and a spiritual enrichment and counselling project, as well as an incentive programme. In just three years Miss Lorna and her team saw a group of students go from not even being able to read three-letter words, to passing their Grade 9 exams and being accepted into high schools and colleges. Miss Lorna is known as the Mother of Trenchtown for all her amazing work in the community getting kids off the streets. She is also one of the craziest and most inspirational people I have ever met. She moved to Trenchtown with only $700 and a determination to do something to change the violent culture. She lived in her office, sleeping on a desk and listening to rats running around at night. One day there was a massive commotion on the street outside and she looked out to see gunmen everywhere. Rather than staying away from it, she ran out onto the street and got in between the two guys at the heart of the trouble who were squaring up to each other. 'You're going to have to shoot me first before anyone else gets killed today,' she told them – and amazingly they backed off. She seemed completely fearless. Even when gang members held a gun to her head and threatened to kill her unless she paid them protection money, she simply knocked the gun away and said, 'Who do you think you are? Jesus?'

The thing that I find so inspiring about both Pastor David and Miss Lorna is that they did not let fear control them, but they put faith into action. They did not see a bad statistic about gun and gang deaths; they got to know individuals, became friends with them and tried to help them out of their particular situations and show them that there was another way. It was not just words: their message was authentic and true and could therefore bring change. We can be tempted to think we need to change in order to reach young people whose experiences are different from ours, but young people see through that immediately. Both Pastor David and Miss Lorna knew they did not have to try to be something they were not. They were themselves and what they offered was a genuine commitment to helping.

Another guy I have come to know on my visits to Trenchtown is Prodigal, who used to be the don (leader) of the aptly named Fatherless Crew. Prodigal's parents died when he was three and he was brought up by his grandmother until she died when he was just thirteen. Left all alone, he joined a gang. There were eleven of them back then; now only he and one other are alive. I asked why he got involved, expecting a long and complicated answer. He gave me the same blunt and startling answer I have heard from young people in the UK: a lack of self-love. How did he get out? He found someone to aspire to: Pastor David.

One of the best ways to support young people is to get to know them, to hang out and spend time with them. Everyone responds to relationship, we are designed for it and it is the way we are wired. I do not know about you, but I have rarely met anyone who does not respond to someone genuinely caring for them. A key thing for almost every person I know who has got out of a gang was to have just one individual who saw them in a different light. We need to look at who individuals can become, not where they are at now. We must always remember that change is possible.

Young people will want to push the boundaries. They will test us and see if we are going to leave them as others in their life have done. It is a real rollercoaster: you might think they are making progress and then they get arrested again. It takes a huge amount of energy, but we need to support people for the long haul, knowing there is no magic solution.

Bearing this in mind, one-off projects are not always that effective. If we parachute in and then leave, all we are doing is reinforcing a young person's experience of lack of consistency. We need to be there through thick and thin, good and bad, and see beyond the situation in front of us. It is so easy not to bother, to think we do not have enough time and energy, to believe we do not have enough to give, or to give in to the fear that these days young people are too dangerous for us to get involved.

We need to be able to offer young people hope. If we give up on them, who else will give them hope? You might have seen the old Michelle Pfeiffer film, *Dangerous Minds*. It is a typical Hollywood production about a teacher turning round failing kids in a tough school, but one scene always sticks in my mind. Pfeiffer is trying to help one of the guys who is being threatened. He turns to her and says, 'How can you save me from my f***ing life?' This is it for so many kids: we are not talking about helping them out of one situation, we are talking about the whole of their lives. They feel that there is no opportunity, no hope. They just cannot see any other way that their lives can be. As Bob Holman, who runs a charity on the Easterhouse Estate in Glasgow, said, 'Inner city wasn't a place, it was a state of mind, and there is a mentality of entrapment, where aspiration and hope are for people who live in another place.'[2]

ROLE MODELS IN THE MEDIA

The current role models seen in the media of people escaping lives of poverty and gang associations are those of rappers or footballers who earn a fortune. Take Dizzee Rascal, who was brought up in London. I know kids can relate to him because the start of his story does not sound too different from their own. His dad died when he was young and his mum worked two jobs to support them. He was excluded from four schools in four years and has hinted at a criminal past including fighting, stealing cars and robbing people. He has been stabbed, he has been arrested, but now he is earning lots of money and selling a massive amount of records. This is someone they can relate to, someone who gives them hope that there is a way out. But are these the most realistic role models? What if you cannot rap or are no good at football? Does that mean the skills that you do have or could develop are not as valuable? We need to give young people more varied and realistic role models, more examples of how to make the most of life whatever your background and gifts.

POSITIVE ROLE MODELS

Are you reading this thinking there is not much you could do? Never think that! The truth is that we can all be role models if we can just get a bit of vision. Vision is the art of seeing the invisible, of seeing what change is possible. If you were able to give just a couple of hours a week to help a young person or a family make lifestyle choices that are wise, you could help turn their lives around completely. Not just make a little difference, but change everything for them. Just a couple of hours a week – that is the difference between one young person feeling uncared for and isolated, getting stuck in a life of crime, and that same young person being able to contribute positively, to have healthy relationships, to learn how to manage their anger, get an education, get a job and have a totally different life. You could be the person who changes everything for them.

At XLP we run a programme called COACH which provides positive role models for young people. The idea is really simple – volunteers who are passionate about making a difference in the lives of young people sign up to give two to three hours a week to coach someone. The volunteers are from all different backgrounds and hold all sorts of roles. We have charity workers, people who run their own business or are in the business world, pastors, security guards, students, life coaches, teachers and even a motivational speaker. Some of our mentors have grown up in similar circumstances to the young people and know the things they are dealing with – the frustrations, fears and obstacles. They know what street life is like and how it can make you feel trapped, so they are desperate to help encourage and demonstrate to the young people that there is a future for them, that they can make something positive out of their lives. Others have come from entirely different backgrounds, but just want to give something back to the community. The one thing they all have in common is that they believe the young people have a lot to give and they want to enable that potential to come to the fore.

The young people who are part of the scheme are referred to us by their school as kids who are particularly at risk from gang life and could really benefit from some one-on-one time with a coach. Many young people feel completely isolated, they do not have a supportive home environment and their friends are in the same situation as they are. Many have been excluded from school, their teachers may have tried to help them but ultimately do not have the time to invest in individuals when there are so many kids in the class with so many different problems. Sometimes the support needed from a coach is incredibly simple. Recently there was one young boy who was not getting up for school, so the first goal set between him and his coach was to get him to attend. His coach phoned him every day for two weeks at 7.30 a.m. to wake him up so he was at school on time and it became a habit that he could then continue himself. Sometimes the activities are rewards, like taking a child to the Science Museum once they have started behaving better at school, or they are aimed at reaching higher goals. One girl wants to become a solicitor, so her coach is organising for them to attend a court case so the girl can see a solicitor in action.

A scheme like COACH gives young people an opportunity to spend one-on-one time with someone and build a relationship with them. It can make all the difference in the world for them to know that there is someone who will listen to them. They need to know that someone cares about them enough to take time out of their busy week and help them work through things that are going on in their lives. They need to know that someone believes in them and will stand by them and help them to be all that they can be – someone who will help them dream about future successes and know they are achievable. The basic hope is that we can help kids stay in the education system in order to give them better job prospects and to keep them out of gangs or support them as they leave the one they are in. It is all about fulfilling their life potential, but something that is also hugely important and often overlooked is that they need a bit of space each week where they get to be a child. So many young people are looking after brothers and sisters at home and earning money to look after their family. They are trying to be adults because adult responsibilities have been put on their shoulders, but they really need a chance to act their age and have fun, away from the stresses and strains of their home lives.

Our hope as well is that this coaching will not only change the lives of the individuals involved, but potentially their families too. Our coaches can provide a link between the young person and their parent or parents. Our team has already met up with kids who have run away from home to try to work through the issues and encourage them to go back. Of the first twenty young people on the scheme, about two thirds do not have a dad at home, but we are in contact with many of their mums in the hope that we

XLP's XLR8 converted double-decker bus

IT Centre at XLP's
XLR8 project

XLP's MTV recording studio van

XLP at Camden's Regent's Park Estate outdoor community day

Breakdancing at Camden's Regent's Park Estate outdoor community day

The XLP sign!

Young people working in the MTV van

Two London estates that benefit from the work of XLP

Daily Stars – winners of the David Idowu Youth Voice Award, presented by Grace Idowu and Patrick Regan

Mutsa – winner of the Arts Showcase Final 2009 with (from left) Simon Hughes MP, Grace Idowu, Patrick Regan and Leo Pswarayi

Trilogy – participants of the Greenwich Showcase 2009

Greenwich and Bexley Arts Showcase programme

Yomi and Ayo – participants of a Southwark Arts Showcase

Total Abyss – winners of the Arts Showcase Final 2008

Patrick Regan
and Sharlene

can work with and support them too. One single mum we are working with said she had been longing to do a college course for years, but did not want to leave her son alone while she went to study. She was so terrified that he would get into trouble that she put her aspirations on hold. Now that one of our coaches can meet up with him, it gives her a few hours a week to pursue her own studies and dreams.

One of the young lads we are working with, Jamie, has an ASBO because he was caught holding a golf club that someone else had just used to smash a sign. The tag means he cannot hang around on his own estate, with the exception of his own flat and his grandma's. He literally cannot loiter between them or even go onto the balcony outside his home. He is on the verge of being excluded from school and is in desperate need of someone to support him so that he stays in the school system. His dad left when he was young and he has been brought up on a council estate near London's South Bank. He lives with his mum and her partner; his sister has moved out and she is suffering from depression to the point of suicide due to bullying. His teachers have stopped giving him homework because they know he will not do it; he is barely engaged with any of his lessons and just runs around the hallways causing disruption. Most of his friends have criminal records and are well known to the police – his best friend is serving time in a Juvenile Detention Unit for a knife-related crime. Many of his family and friends are immersed in football hooliganism and often get involved in fights and riots while supporting their team. It is not hard to see the spiral his life would take if no one intervened. But now one of our coaches meets with Jamie once a week to keep him in school and stop him from being excluded. So far the coaching has helped keep Jamie out of a gang fight that led to two of his mates being stabbed, and his mentor has given him the confidence to stay in school to get his GCSEs.

This highlights the need for us to get alongside people like Jamie when they are young. In the words of JaJa, a former member of the PDC: 'When I wanted to go on the straight and narrow there wasn't much support. When the kids go bad, do crime, go to jail and finally realise there's more to life than guns and drugs, where do they go for support? Who is there for them? It's just us against the world. We need help. Please help us.'[3]

Left alone, boys like Jamie and JaJa are highly likely to follow their mates and end up with a criminal record. This wrecks their chances of getting a job in the future, pointing them further towards a life of crime. If we intervene, show them someone cares, talk to them about their options, expand their horizons and support them to make a decent life for themselves, we can help them create a positive future.

6

Nothing Stops a Bullet Like a Job

They had money and drove around in cars. I did stuff for them – delivered stuff, drugs I suppose. Some school mates have joined gangs. They were attracted to the cars and the money. You can get girls. You see the older guys and they're living it up. It's one way of living that seems good – money and respect . . .

(*South Manchester gang member*)[1]

People trace the roots of modern gangs back to the 1980s when there was massive economic and social change. While many prospered, the most deprived communities became even poorer. Since then gangs have sprung up most commonly in socially deprived areas, essentially in our big cities like London, Manchester, Liverpool and Glasgow. For many living on estates in these places, worldly wealth is only a stone's throw away from them. If you stand in the towers of London's Aylesbury Estate, you can see the imposing buildings in the City of London, full of successful business people earning their six-figure salaries. Just up the road from many people who live below the poverty line are huge houses protected by expensive alarm systems, three or four flashy cars sitting on the driveway. For some there is no getting away from the wealth divide, it is in their face, reminding them of what they do not have and what society has been telling them for years would make their life successful.

The statistics are quite alarming for young people growing up in deprived areas. A child born in Lambeth is likely to die eight years before their counterpart in the wealthier area of Kensington and Chelsea. They are 50 per cent more likely to be born into a single-parent family, and have less than a 40 per cent chance of achieving five GCSEs grades A–C. There is a 20 per cent chance that they will get no qualifications at all. The probability of becoming a problem drug user is five times as high in Lambeth, and the likelihood of teenage conception is four times as high as for those in Kensington and Chelsea. They are also far more likely to become both a victim and a perpetrator of violent crime.[2] Elsewhere the facts can be even more shocking, with the life expectancy of a child born in the poorer Calton area of Glasgow being fifty-four years, while for those in the more affluent Lenzie area in the same city it is eighty-two years.[3]

UK youth unemployment is rising above the European average,[4] and in our inner cities the situation is particularly bad. For example, London saw a 33 per cent increase in youth unemployment in the space of four years,[5] and in one London borough where XLP works, only one young person in four is employed. With the general economic picture not predicting a bright future or a decrease in these figures, young people are looking for alternative models of living. If they do not have an income and a sense of purpose from a job, they will look for it elsewhere. Add to this the growing problem that today's generation wants everything now, and the way the media push the need to keep up your image with designer labels and the latest technology, and you find them looking for quick solutions to make cash. Selling drugs is one of the fastest ways to make money and is common for gang members.

Even from a young age they will be offered money by the Elders to take drugs to buyers or to stash drugs when police come along. The risk is something they get used to and the rewards seem far greater than those offered by the job market.

THE VALUE OF AN EDUCATION

With the pressure on schools to 'succeed', a strong emphasis is placed on teachers helping those kids who are just below average to raise their grades and pass so that the school's statistics are good. But if you are in the bottom 20 per cent and the school does not see much hope of you ever passing, you may well be overlooked. If you fail to get an education, your prospects for employment are slim, your hopes for the future even slimmer.

The majority of gang members I have spoken to do not have an education and the story is often pretty similar. With family problems at home, and frustrations and anger they do not know how to deal with, many young guys act up and get violent, meaning teachers cannot deal with them in school. Some have been excluded so many times and from such a young age that they are actually a couple of years behind the rest of their peers in their learning. At secondary school, disruptive pupils are often sent to a Pupil Referral Unit (PRU) in their borough with the aim that they can receive extra help there, both with their school work and ideally also with the issues that led to their expulsion. In theory the pupil is then able to return to school to take their GCSEs. In reality, many schools do not want to re-admit teenagers who have been difficult in the past, because they are worried about their pass rates and being labelled as a failing school. As a result, many young people see the PRU as a form of punishment rather than an alternative to help them stay in education. There is a definite stigma attached to the units and young people feel as though they have been labelled as stupid if they are sent there (even if they are sent there for behavioural rather than educational issues). Pupils often talk about going to 'the Centre' instead of the PRU because they are embarrassed.

Some recognise the PRU as their last chance. They are desperate to do well and try really hard to get their work done. Others see it as another badge to prove how tough they are – they have been kicked out of school, continue to cause disruption and still no one can control them. They might act as if they do not care and they would rather be anywhere else rather than in a classroom, but the truth is, expulsion is isolating and alienating. It is another rejection; another person or institution that says you do not belong and you are not wanted. Some young people have learned so many negative behaviour patterns that even the additional support offered in a PRU is not enough. They stop attending and spend their days on the streets, with no qualifications and no hopes of a satisfying job to motivate them. All they have is a desperate desire to fit in.

That is one of the reasons why we see helping young people to stay in education as a priority in helping decrease gang culture. Having qualifications, having good prospects, finding a sense of purpose and belonging both at school and at work can make all the difference. One of the first things the XLP team got involved in was going into schools and sitting with kids who have difficulty reading. The one-on-one time that was so easy for the team to give made all the difference for some of these children, who had no one else to really help them grasp this basic skill. It is always a reminder to me that we might feel as if the contribution we make is small (sitting for half an hour a week with someone does not exactly feel like saving the world), but it can change someone's life. Setting them up with the ability to read gives them confidence to go on and achieve more, but without this skill, there is little hope of them getting anywhere at school and in the job market.

This cannot be stressed enough: getting young people to stay in education so they can go into good employment is absolutely key to giving them a future that does not involve gangs and crime.

THE FREEDOM WRITERS

While I was in Los Angeles doing research for *Dying to Belong*, we went to a place called the Freedom Writers Institute and spent some time with its founder, Erin Gruwell. In the early 1990s Erin started teaching a class at Woodrow Wilson High School in Long Beach, California, a class that had been written off as a group that would never graduate – a bunch of delinquents who were unteachable. The class represented a multitude of gangs. The only things the pupils had in common were that they hated each other, hated school and hated their teacher. Not what most people would consider an ideal starting post for a white, middle-class woman.

But Erin was not put off. She found ways to help the class recognise their similarities and gave them books to read, written by teenagers so that they could connect with them. They started with *The Diary of Anne Frank* and began to realise that if they could relate to a little girl who lived on the other side of the world fifty years ago, they could certainly relate to the other pupils in the classroom. Next they read *Zlata's Diary* – the story of a young girl living in Sarajevo during the Bosnian war. Again they related to the violence she saw, motivated by ethnic and religious differences.

Erin also used journalling as a way to allow the pupils to express themselves. They began the journals anonymously; they were not being graded, just given an opportunity to explain what was going on in their lives. Their writing told of their everyday problems:

gangs, violence, abuse, death, anorexia, dyslexia, love, weight issues, divorce, suicide. Nothing was off limits. They began to call themselves The Freedom Writers.

Gradually the classroom became a safe place for everyone, a community where they could share their stories, laugh and cry without being judged. The methods Erin employed were so successful that all 150 pupils graduated from high school and went on to attend college, many as the first in their family ever to do so. Helping them see that they could graduate was a huge step forward, as it meant they all let go of the negative voices from their past telling them they would not amount to anything.

One of the girls in the class, Maria, says, 'What was different with Ms G. was that regardless of what we thought about ourselves, what we believed to be true, she believed something completely different. That we could put behind ourselves any choices that we'd made in our lives before, and that it was the choices we made from that point on that mattered. And she just stuck it out, she didn't give up on us, ever.'[6]

Their story was so incredible and their diary entries so raw and moving that they were made into a book called *The Freedom Writers' Diary*. In turn this was made into a film starring Hilary Swank. The film shows a scene where Erin invites each pupil to make a symbolic 'toast for change' – an acknowledgement of the fact that they can have hopes and dreams for their lives. In that scene one girl says she always thought she would be pregnant before she was sixteen like her mum, but the class had made her see it did not have to be that way. One guy thought he would be dead before he reached eighteen, but Erin made him realise he could have a future. And so the stories go on. Having someone believe in them made these teenagers, whom most considered 'lost', realise that they did not have to live up to the stereotypes or the things they thought were inevitable in their own lives. Erin and the Freedom Writers started the Freedom Writers Foundation, a charity dedicated to recreating the success of their classroom for other young people throughout the country.

I had coffee with Maria (represented by 'Eva' in the film), who was a third-generation gang leader. From the age of five she knew to duck when she heard a car slow down, in case it was a drive-by shooting. She found a sense of belonging in the gang and did not believe she would live to see her seventeenth birthday. 'Why would I?' she said simply. 'I thought no one who looks like me ever gets anywhere and no one was looking out for me.' When Erin suggested that the class read *The Diary of Anne Frank*, Maria felt she could totally relate to the Jewish girl who was forced into hiding. Maria says, 'Anne Frank says she felt like a bird in a cage, wishing she could fly away. That summed me up; I knew exactly how she felt.'

LEVELLING AN UNEVEN PLAYING FIELD

Talking to Erin made it clear to me that education is the only way to level an uneven playing field for our young people. They may grow up in poverty, looking out over the wealth of others, but if we can arm them with an education we can give them hope for their future.

Erin also says that finding texts young people can relate to is key. One thing I have found is that if a teenager is learning to read, they are still given books that would be meant for a five-year-old. Being illiterate is embarrassing enough without being asked to read 'the cat sat on the mat' type of stuff. As Erin says, we have to find ways to make the content in the classroom relevant to where young people are at if we are to keep their interest and help them really succeed.

Had Erin walked into that classroom and seen only what other people saw, she too would have written off the class. They did not seem to care, so why should she? But she saw something else; she saw what they could be. There is one moving scene in the film where the class have been asked to grade their own papers. One boy, Andre, has given himself an F and Erin pulls him aside to ask him why. 'It's what I feel I deserve,' he says, looking away from her. 'This F is a "f**k you" to me and to everyone in class,' Erin tells him. 'I know what you're up against. We're all of us up against something so you better make up your mind. Because until you have the balls to look me straight in the eye and tell me this is all you deserve, I am not letting you fail. Even if that means coming round to your house every night until you finish the work. I see who you are. Do you understand me? I can see you. And you are not failing.'

Erin walked into a classroom and saw individuals. She believed they each had value, every person in that classroom had something positive to contribute to society, and her belief not only changed their lives but the lives of many others who have been impacted by the work of the Freedom Writers.

JOBS NOT JAILS

For some it seems that it is too late. They have missed out on an education for whatever reason and through bad choice have got a criminal record. The chances of them finding regular employment seem slim, so is it too late to help them? One inspiring person I met is Father Greg Boyle, or Father G as he is more commonly known, and he would say that it is never too late. His work in Los Angeles is all about helping gang members get into employment and his mission statement reads:

Jobs not Jails: Homeboy Industries assists at-risk and formerly
gang-involved youth to become positive and contributing
members of society through job placement, training and
education.

It all started in 1988 when Father G, a Jesuit priest, was so
concerned about the number of kids dying and the unmet needs
of young people going into gangs that he began a mission called
'Jobs For a Future'. The aim was to provide positive alternatives to
gangs. So he and the community set up a primary school and a
day-care programme and helped get young people into legitimate
employment. What started as a relatively small community project
has grown to become an amazing initiative called Homeboy
Industries that has helped literally thousands of gang members
turn their lives around. It is now the largest gang intervention
programme in America.

The idea is simple and is based on Father G's often quoted
phrase, 'Nothing stops a bullet like a job'. His experience of talking to many gang members, even those very seriously involved,
was that they wanted to get off the streets but they just saw no
way out. Knowing how hard it is for ex-offenders to find employment, Father G set up his own social enterprise allowing for training and work experience and providing a living wage. They run
all sorts of successful businesses now, including a bakery, land-
scaping, maintenance, silk-screening and selling Homeboy
Industries merchandise. A couple of years ago they opened
Homegirl Café, providing jobs for girls too. They also offer part-
time roles to under-seventeens who need work.

Such is the sense of family and belonging at these enterprises
that old rivals now work side by side. Louis Perez, Senior
Navigator at Homeboy Industries, said, 'I work with guys that I

shot at before, I work with guys that at one time I tried to kill, now they're my friends and we talk about everything. Homeboys is my family.'

HOPE

Father G says that 'hopeful kids don't join gangs', and that is what we are talking about when we look at the issue of poverty. Take Marsha, who works at the Homegirl Café. She was raised in foster homes and abused when she was little. Her family were in gangs and she was only ten when she first got arrested. She says that when she was little she wanted to be a paediatrician, but her step-mum kept telling her it would never happen. 'She'd tell me all the time and so I thought I couldn't be one.' If, instead of telling her what she *could not* do, someone had encouraged Marsha that she *could* be a paediatrician if she worked hard in school, maybe her life would have turned out differently.

One of our youth workers at XLP, Chris, told me about a boy called Neil he worked with at a PRU who had been excluded from school since he was in primary education. Neil had missed so much schooling that, at the age of fourteen, he still could not read very well, and to him, the idea getting any kind of education seemed such a huge mountain to climb that he often made out that he did not care. He was dealing drugs from the age of fifteen and was often involved in football firm fighting. Chris stayed opti-mistic that things could change for Neil and spent time asking him what he wanted to do in life. Neil felt that the thing he could do well was to be a good dad, and that was his goal. Through the time they spent together, Chris was able to help Neil see that to achieve his goal he would need to get some kind of qualifications in order to get a job and be able to provide for his family. Chris stuck with him, making him see that he could learn to read and could slowly build towards his goal. Chris said, 'It's hard for young people to have hope when they're looking at your life and thinking they will never achieve the things that some of us take for granted. Neil lived so close to me, but our experiences and upbringing were completely different. One of my main goals when working with Neil was to give him a picture of what his life could be and to show him that with some work it was within his grasp.'

Without the positive and consistent influence of someone like Chris, so many kids face life with a lack of hope. They may start off with dreams and ambitions, but people tell them it is never going to happen and soon enough they believe it and live out the fact that they have nothing positive to offer the world. What is the point in getting all your homework done and paying attention in class if it is never going to get you where you want to go? They are left with little education and see only two choices ahead of them: slogging their guts out doing two jobs a day like their mums and still only just scraping by, or joining a gang and earning hundreds or thousands of pounds a week selling drugs and doing crime. People like Father G and his team offer an alternative and not only *talk* about giving people hope, they put their money where their mouth is and give hope itself. They give people training, a job and a chance to change their lives – and that is hope in action.

Homeboy Industries understand, too, that many ex-gang members need other types of support in order to stay in their jobs and keep going with their positive life decisions. To this end they provide mental health counselling, legal services and twelve-step programmes to help rehabilitate alcohol and drug addicts. Another vital service they offer is tattoo removal. This might seem strange, but it can actually save someone's life. Gangs use tattoos as ways of affiliating themselves to each other and showing the crimes they have committed. If someone is trying to leave a gang but still bears the marks, a rival could easily shoot them, thinking they were still part of their old gang. It is also a really good way for an ex-gang member to demonstrate that they are moving on and leaving their past behind them. All of these things are offered for free to anyone who wants and needs help.

I also loved Father G's mentality that we should keep giving people as many chances as they need. Everyone he works with knows that if they mess up, Homeboy Industries will still be there for them when they are ready to try again. But the reality is that having people believe in them makes the employees so much more likely to succeed and not mess it up in the first place.

UK PROGRAMMES

Here in the UK signs of similar projects are starting to appear. HM Prison High Down in Sutton, Surrey, for example, has opened a fully functioning restaurant (called The Clink) inside the prison that is operated entirely by prisoners. The prisoners volunteer to be trained in food preparation and work towards qualifications, while the restaurant encourages bookings from individuals, companies and organisations who are interested in supporting the offenders when they have finished their sentence and return to the community. The man behind it, Chef Alberto Crisci, said he wanted The Clink to help change the public's perception of prisoners and for it to be 'the sound of chains being broken for men who want, and have worked hard to deserve, a second chance at life'.

Charities like Pecan, based in south London, also work with ex-offenders, aiming to get them into sustainable employment within eight weeks of leaving prison. They help them with training, finding voluntary placements and job seeking, as well as providing them with mentoring support – all to reduce their chances of re-offending and to help them as they reintegrate into society.

POVERTY OF ASPIRATION

I have learned a huge lesson from seeing organisations like Homeboys and Pecan in action: we have to give young people hope at a time when they seem bankrupt of hope. As Jules Pipe, Mayor of Hackney, said, 'It's extraordinary the narrowness of vision that some of these young people have. People living in Hackney who have never been to the West End, let alone further afield . . . And that probably is a huge issue behind what is driving [involvement in gangs] . . . poverty of aspiration. That's actually far more a factor in this than alcohol or drugs.'[7]

Through gang lifestyles young people are limiting their choices about education, about work and even about where they can spend their time. We work with kids on an estate that backs onto one of London's most famous parks and yet most of them have never even been there. If we do not give them hope about what positive things they can achieve with their lives, they will embrace the things that will eventually destroy them. We have to see that they can be more than they are and find all the ways we can to support, train and equip them to do it. We have to find ways to give them a sense of purpose, pride and achievement. We have to be there for them if they make mistakes and we cannot give up on them.

7

Fear

We need to find out what makes people feel safer in a gang than out of one.

(*Sir Ian Blair, former Commissioner of the Metropolitan Police*) [1]

Of the young people who report carrying a knife, an incredible 85 per cent of them say they only do so for protection. This highlights a growing trend: young people in areas where gangs are rife are seeing friends, neighbours, family members and classmates being stabbed and shot. They are left with only one conclusion: they need some kind of protection. They carry a weapon in the hope that it will deter other people from attacking them and they hope never to have to use it. While it is still only a small percentage of young people who carry a knife, it is important to note that the number of kids *outside* gangs carrying them is on the increase. We are not talking about hardened young people who are immersed in gang culture, we are talking about scared teenagers, fearful of being attacked. When people are scared and think they could be the next victim, they will go to extreme lengths to prevent that from happening. Media headlines about everyone carrying knives can aggravate the fear, and we will look at the impact of this in more depth in chapter 9.

Kelly, who used to be on the edge of gangs, told me that hearing about other young people carrying knives led her to carry a kitchen knife if she had to walk through a rough area. She said, 'I'm not that type of girl, but I wanted to feel safe, especially if I was in a different area. I wanted to feel protected and that meant either being in a gang or carrying a knife.' One of the XLP youth workers, Anna, told me that on one estate she met a mother who has removed all the kitchen knives from her house and now uses normal cutlery to cut and carve meat. She had found that her son was hiding her knives around the house so he could easily grab one at any time, and she felt the only option was to rid the house of all of them.

For some, carrying a knife or gun is a rash decision, enhanced by the peer pressure of their gang egging them on. For others it seems like their only form of defence. By carrying a weapon they risk a prison sentence of up to five years, but that seems an acceptable gamble when the alternative is being defenceless and losing your life. The truth is that for many, the everyday fear of gangs and what they can do to you is far greater than the fear of being caught and going to prison.

Although young people may be carrying weapons for protection, the more guns and knives there are around, the more stabbings and shootings happen, whether they are premeditated or not. I will never forget a story I heard about a headmaster who had been a youth worker. He was helping with a youth event when a lad called Nathan turned up one evening with a knife. Nathan got it out to show his mate Daniel, who jokingly held it up to Nathan's throat. They were just messing about when a third lad, completely unaware of the knife being there, accidentally pushed into the back of Daniel. There was no warning and no time to get the knife out of the way; it went straight through Nathan's main vein and just moments later he died in the teacher's arms. What had seemed like a laugh to Nathan had resulted in his tragic death. In court the judge simply said that if you live by the sword, you die by the sword.

THE POLICE AND THE WALL OF SILENCE

In most parts of the country, if we have a problem we can go to the police. We trust them to help us, but in many areas that confidence does not exist. A recent BBC poll of teenagers showed that 44 per cent felt the police were unable to protect them from violent crime.[2] For gang members there is a code of silence. People do not speak up about what has happened to them and they do not give evidence about things they have seen either. Of course it all revolves around the fear of reprisals – the fear of what will happen to them if they do speak. Recently in London a man was stabbed through the skull at 5 p.m. outside a major supermarket. Despite this taking place on a busy road at rush hour with lots of shoppers and passers-by, the police could not find anyone who was willing to admit to seeing anything.

You can imagine how frustrating it is for the police to hit this kind of brick wall every time they try to do their job, and how devastating it is for victims and their loved ones when no one is ever brought to justice. Beverley Thomas, whose daughter Charlene was accidentally killed by a gang in a drive-by shooting in Birmingham in 2003, said, 'There were people there who saw and became blind or who heard and became deaf.' Mr Mirfield from the West Midlands Police said this 'wall of silence' made their task incredibly difficult. 'The people we were dealing with, the gangsters, the way in which they live their lives, makes any such investigation extremely difficult. They try and rule with fear and intimidation. It is a culture . . . in which no one talks to the police come what may. Anybody who does is considered an informant or a grass.' This, of course, leads to gangs feeling that they are invincible – they can shoot who they like, commit what crimes they like and get away with it, because people are too scared to talk.[3]

But in a number of significant cases these problems have been overcome with a lot of hard work and determination. In Moss Side, Manchester, police encountered this wall of silence when trying to solve the murder of fifteen-year-old Jessie James, who was said to be an innocent victim, caught in the wrong place at the wrong time. In order for witnesses to testify, they held the inquest in a court usually reserved for terrorist trials. From a secret location, witnesses gave statements that were relayed to the coroner in court via video, their voices and faces distorted to the point that no one would know whether they were male or female, young or old.[4]

Members of a gang were also brought to justice over the death of seventeen-year-old Jamie Robe in Rotherhithe when MP Simon Hughes got involved. Police and Jamie's father, Stuart, had spent months on the case, looking for witnesses of the attack that had happened outside a kebab shop. Stuart received death threats and abuse and when Simon Hughes got involved a contract was put out on his life. Undeterred, Hughes spoke to witnesses such as the kebab shop owners and encouraged them to speak to police, even though they had spent the year since the attack denying they had seen anything. In court the witnesses wore balaclavas and boiler suits and stood behind a screen to avoid being identified. More than two years after Jamie was beaten to death in the street, three men were finally convicted and sentenced to life imprisonment.

STOP AND SEARCH

Under the Police & Criminal Evidence Act (1984), the police have the right to stop and search members of the public for weapons. While many understand why this is necessary, for young black men in particular it is a source of real anger. They get stopped a disproportionate number of times just because of their age and colour. One young guy told me he was constantly getting stopped and, while he understood why the police had to do it, he said the manner in which they did it left him humiliated, even though he had done nothing wrong. He lives in an area where there is widespread drug use, but as he said, 'That's just where I live. I can't help that and it doesn't mean that I'm carrying anything.'

One issue that may contribute to the problems between police and kids in inner-city areas is that the racial make-up of the police force does not reflect the community it is working in. For example, in Peckham you get a predominantly white police force turning up to deal with issues in a predominantly black African-Caribbean area. In some parts of LA this is something they have worked hard to redress, so that there is less of a racial divide at moments of intense conflict.

Of course gang members and people serious about carrying weapons get wise to the rules of initiatives like stop and search anyhow. As mentioned earlier, they may use girls and younger kids to carry weapons and drugs for them, as they are unlikely to be stopped. They also carry screwdrivers and craft knives, which they can do legally, but can still use to inflict a lot of pain on someone. The latest trend I have heard of is people breaking CDs and using the sharp edges as a weapon that can do serious damage. Increasingly there are also reports of gangs using dogs like bull terriers and bull mastiffs to inflict damage on other people. It is not illegal to own one of these dogs, but they create fear in those who see them and can wound someone easily. In fact, in one year, accident and emergency units in London reported a 119 per cent increase in the cases of under-eighteens being admitted with dog bites.[5]

RELUCTANT GANG MEMBERS

For many, the only way to find protection and a feeling of relative safety is to become part of a gang. As Elijah said, he was beaten up just because of where he came from, but once he joined a gang, he did not have to live in fear any more – he had people there to protect him. For many it seems to be safer to be in a gang than to be outside one. It lowers the risk of being attacked. Some young people have hung out with the same group of guys most of their lives, and then they find that the group has become more and more involved in criminal activity. Even if they would not have become involved in crime alone, they end up going along with their friends because there seems to be no other choice. For others, just living on the wrong estate means that a gang will try to get them involved and not leave them any choice in the matter. In John Pitts' study *Reluctant Gangsters*, he says, 'If the local gang asks someone on the estate to do something, like a street robbery, they know they must do it or suffer the consequences.' Another Youth Offending Team worker said, 'There was a brother and a sister; he was fifteen and she was fourteen. Never been in trouble. They told them to do a robbery. But they said no. So they beat him up and raped her.'[6]

I heard of two brothers on one estate who were both competing in martial arts events all over Europe, and so a local gang wanted to recruit them, knowing they would be excellent street fighters. The brothers were not interested, but found their house was fire-bombed by the rejected gang. One of the boys was stabbed and the other bottled – a terrifying example of what can happen to kids who say no to gangs.

GETTING OUT

Things are even harder for anyone trying to leave the gang lifestyle. Other gangs still see you as a rival and your own former gangmates can feel disrespected by your exit from the crew, so they will be after you too. Some say the only way to leave a gang is to leave the area entirely, but that is not easy if you are a teenager with no job, no money and nowhere else to go. One girl said, 'When you're in there's no way out. You could walk away with one finger missing, a bullet hole in your leg, be stabbed in the face or cut from ear to ear.'[7]

The police told me about one boy, Ivan, who fell into a gang at his school. Being bigger and more athletic than lots of the guys, he became one of the leaders, earned himself a reputation and soon found he had a following. Ivan was arrested for attacking people and stealing, along with fellow gang members. As he chatted to the police officers it became clear that Ivan wanted to leave the gang, but could not see how he could do it; he knew they would turn on him if he tried. During a home visit, he showed the officers his stab wounds: one on his chest, one on his head and one on his leg. The solution was actually relatively simple in this case. The police gave Ivan details of local activities that were available, like football put on by the local council and football club. Ivan said having a reason to be somewhere else stopped him having to explain to the gang members why he was not out stealing and fighting with them.

It is also reported that some young people who want to leave gangs are eager to get themselves police tags. It may sound strange, but having a tag means they have to be home by a certain time, so they have a reason to tell their gang they cannot be out with them. It is like a 'get out of jail free card'. They are still respected, as they have proved themselves in the past, but they are able to walk away from the gang's activities without having the gang turn on them.

MANNY'S STORY

For many people in Glasgow, gangs and violence are just a way of life, with generations of men belonging to the same gangs. Often you get classified as belonging to a gang just because of where you live, whether you want to be involved or not. My first experience of the extreme violence was when I was just seven years old. I had gone to the Saturday matinee at the cinema and on the way out there was a huge fight going on in the streets outside. As I made my way to the bus I saw the battle going on. There was a man lying in the gutter with an army bayonet in his back. Then a guy ran in front of me and someone behind him put an axe to his head. I was terrified.

Just a couple of years later I was caught up in it again. I was on the street outside my home playing football with a friend when a mob of two hundred guys from a neighbouring gang came onto our street carrying swords, metal bars and axes. As they came through they smashed every car on the way. My friend and I ran – these guys were all seventeen or eighteen and we were just nine. We rushed towards some garages to hide, but as we got there we saw this guy standing with a fireman's axe coming right up to his chin. As the two-hundred-strong crowd ran towards him, he picked up the axe and ran at them all while another group emerged from the nearby woods. The guy with the axe had been there alone so the rest of his gang – the PAKA – could take the others by surprise. Eventually the coppers turned up, but both gangs joined forces to turn on them. They were hell bent on violence and nothing was going to stop them.

My friend and I became mascots for the PAKA, which stood for Pursue And Kill All. I got my identity from being with this gang. They gave me a new nickname, Mad Manny, and they would use us as bait. We would go and start on someone and as soon as they lifted a hand to us, everyone else would jump in. We would go to a local dance hall to fight and I regularly saw people slashed with blades, stabbed with chisels through the head and killed. I was so well known that at the age of twelve I had eighteen-year-olds after me. One time I even stole two swords from my brother, which I took to school when I heard another gang was after me. Of course I got caught, but I managed to persuade the Head they were not mine. When these guys came looking for me at lunch I was empty handed and desperately looking around for something to use to attack them with. When they reached me, though, they just shook my hand and said they had heard about me. I was getting a real reputation. That was such a buzz; I loved being recognised. Every time I went into Glasgow, people would keep stopping me to say hello and show me respect.

At the age of seventeen I started selling drugs to everyone and smoking them myself. It got to the point where I was stoned 24-7. I was fighting nearly every single day, either with people in school or others in gangs. I became the leader of the young PAKA. One boy tried to take me on one time while we were sitting in a mate's house drinking. I went to stab him in the face, but someone pushed me and it went into his neck. He survived, but he never challenged my leadership again and everyone else was too terrified.

When I was nineteen my old man got cancer and I had to nurse him through the last few months of his life.

Around the same time a mate of mine had a motorbike accident when he was picking up some hash for me. He was hit by one car and knocked from his bike, then another car hit him, crushing his head. I went to the hospital and he was in a coma; they said he would die that night. I started questioning my life and the violence all around me. I tried to walk away and distance myself from it, but it has followed me around ever since. Because of my reputation there was always someone looking to recruit me to their gang; even the paramilitary asked me to join them. I was so used to violence that if someone started on me I did not know how to walk away. Even in my twenties I got into a fight at a bus stop. Two guys tried to hit me with a broken vodka bottle, so I got a butcher's knife and when one guy ran at me it went straight into his chest. I pulled the blade out and stabbed him again and again.

Even after I was married and had children I was still getting involved in violence. I had people knocking on my door with weapons, threatening me while my kids were in bed. One time I had to send my family to a safe house while I sat for three days with a sawn-off shotgun waiting for these guys to show up. Another time I remember being in a drug dealer's house when my wife was pregnant with our fourth child, and they were threatening that what they were about to do to me would send her into labour. I knew they meant they were planning on killing me. I was thirty-four and still getting threats. Two years later I moved from Glasgow and it still took a number of years before I felt free of my violent past. I had become a Christian when I was younger, but struggled to fit into church. For many of the people there, they were dealing with issues like how to pay the mortgage each month, whereas I was trying to stay off drugs and keep away from the violence that could lead to me being killed. One of the key turning points for me was when another guy came alongside me. Instead of judging me, he listened to me, supported me and did not try to make me fit into a culture that was not me. I needed that stability and consistency and it helped me make some positive lifestyle choices and begin to deal with the complex things that had happened in my life. I do not want to glamorise anything that I have done; I truly regret it. Being in a gang was like a curse that has followed me around my whole life and it has taken me many years to get free.

8

Anger

Anger flares up when someone looks at someone else in the wrong way . . . Someone makes a comment and the next thing someone else is dead. It's crazy.

(*Barry Mizen, whose son Jimmy was killed during an argument in a bakery in South East London in May 2008*)

When we hear of young people getting involved in violent acts we can wonder what on earth fuels them: how can they behave like that, particularly over something as small as a look? What seems to be the case is that many of our young people are boiling over with anger and are ready to explode at the slightest provocation. Anyone who has witnessed gang violence will say that often people's rage goes from 0 to 60 in seconds. One minute they are calm, the next they feel disrespected, a knife has been pulled and someone is bleeding. Many young people are living on the edge with few healthy outlets for their rage and no conflict resolution skills, so their anger is unleashed randomly and often with appalling consequences.

In reference to Britain's youth, some politicians have asked, 'What have they got to be angry about?' You probably have a good idea, from some of the issues we have already looked at in this book, that many young people are trying to deal with impossible situations, such as:

- living in poverty;
- growing up without a dad and no positive male role model;
- seeing their dad beat their mum and feeling powerless to do anything about it;
- seeing friends, family members and neighbours being shot, stabbed and killed;
- feeling as if there is no hope for their future;
- suffering physical, verbal and sexual abuse;
- dealing with the fact that having a criminal record means they struggle to find work, even if they are desperate to turn their lives around;
- feeling let down by their school or teachers;
- feeling rejected by friends, family or even society;
- seeing their parents working long hours and yet still struggling to make a living;
- the responsibility of looking after their younger siblings while their parents are not around.

Sadly, there are plenty of things for them to feel angry about and few outlets for them to vent their feelings safely.

We have to remember that from a very young age kids have a sense of justice. How many times have you heard the phrase 'it's not fair' from a child? Young people grow up seeing what others have – whether that is a secure family unit, popularity among their peers, the ability to do well at school, or enough money to get the latest clothes. As I said earlier, some kids growing up below the poverty line on certain estates live so close to people living in plenty that they cannot get away from what they do not have.

Joe said, 'You see someone in clothes you don't have, your mum doesn't make enough money and she's split up with your dad. There's all these kids with new trainers, wearing the latest shirts and jackets. That alone frustrates you. It makes you want to rob someone, get their phone and sell it so you can get something new. There's no way to get what you want except robbing someone.'

John Sutherland, Superintendent of Islington Borough Police, explained, 'Some of our young people don't have the emotional resilience or intelligence to deal with their problems in any other way than to use their fists, a knife or a gun. If you've had a balanced upbringing and you're faced with conflict you may have a choice of, say, three or four ways you might respond. For kids who come from difficult backgrounds, they are lucky if they have two choices. One is anger and it's the most common one; many young people can't seem to deal with their issues in any other way.'

Others have pointed out how much anger can control you: 'Anger is addictive, it makes me feel strong. It makes me believe that "I am right!" and that being right is what matters most. It builds a wall that, I desperately hope, will keep marauders out. It becomes so intoxicating that I am constantly primed and ready to get some more and sends me strutting self-righteously down the street, head held high and heart beating double time. I may even come to the point of believing that I can't live without it. But anger only begets more anger, as violence begets violence. My tolerance to it increases, a little is too much, and a lot is never enough.'[1]

I have met so many people who are like this. Take David. At three years old he saw his dad trying to push his mum through a broken glass door; he saw the blood and listened to his mum's cries and sobs for it to stop, helpless to do anything. As he grew up, such fights between his parents were the norm and David was regularly beaten by his dad. His uncles would come round and in volatile arguments would draw knives on each other. There was always violence in David's home, so is it any wonder that as he grew up he sorted out his issues with his fists? As he says himself, he knew no other way to get his point across.

RETALIATION

One of the key factors that seems to perpetuate gang violence is retaliation for an offence committed against the gang. Nadhir, a young lad the XLP team know through our schools and mentoring work, told us that when his friend was stabbed recently, he knew about it within hours even though he had no phone and was at home himself because of his tag curfew. People were giving him information about it on MSN, speculating about who did it and feeding him information so that he could be the ringleader of the inevitable reprisal. The way he spoke, it was as though the retaliation was just inevitable; it was almost something that he would be involved in outside his own control.

Of course when someone dies, the anger and the desire for revenge increases tenfold. I remember chatting to Omar, a school pupil in Trenchtown who had recently lost both his father and his uncle in a gang war. I was shocked by the lack of emotion in his voice as he told me of their deaths, and his eyes were blank, staring straight through me. I asked him whether there was any counselling or anyone for him to talk to when he was bereaved and he said there was not. 'How do you feel?' I asked. His eyes caught mine for the first time as he said, 'Angry.' His teacher told me Omar is now himself seen walking with gunmen.

NATHANIEL'S STORY

I came to the UK from Nigeria when I was just six months old. My dad had been working as a doctor but his qualifications weren't accepted here so he went off travelling and we never saw him. When I was at primary school my mum worked two jobs so sometimes we wouldn't see her for days at a time. My sister was fourteen and she would get us ready for school, do all the cooking and the cleaning. My mum cared for us and wanted to be around but we needed the money so she had to take the work. My brother was very good at football and I loved it too. He started playing professionally and there was an expectation on me to follow in his footsteps especially when I became the team captain in Year 8. I was pretty well behaved in school, I did well in my exams and so got some leeway and always managed to slide out of trouble if I did anything wrong.

When I was fifteen my uncle came to stay with us for a while. With no dad around he became a big figure in my life for the year he was there. One day he was gone and a few months later we found out he'd become addicted to drugs and had been killed; his body was found three weeks after his death, dumped in a rubbish bin. I was so angry that he'd been taken away from me and angry with my mum for not telling me the details of what had happened even though I was too young to handle it. I didn't tell anyone what had happened; I kept all my feelings bottled up and I started hanging out with a bad crowd. I felt like my uncle's death was a good excuse to be bad and though I still managed to do well in my exams, I started getting into lots of fights because I couldn't control my temper. I got suspended for fighting my best friend over a game of 'penny up'. Over the summer holidays a friend of mine from the estate I lived on was killed. After getting into a fight he was stabbed outside a nightclub. That added to my anger – I was still reeling from my uncle's death less than two years before. My friend's death brought me closer to my other friends on the streets and as I spent more time with them I started following what they were doing and stealing phones with them. I've never been one to follow the crowd though and thought if I was going to steal then I wanted to be the biggest and the best. I hadn't been looking for a reputation but I got one anyway and then I had to keep it up.

Someone offered me some weed to sell and I started making quite a bit of money. I also began messing around with cars and realised I could fix them up so I started doing that and making even more cash which I saved. I applied for college and wanted to do performing arts as I loved being centre stage. Everyone there came from totally different backgrounds from me so they treated me like the college gangster. Knives and guns were normal to me; they were the accessories you needed if you were robbing from people on the streets. Over the summer holidays I got stopped by the police – they were suspicious as I was wearing a big gold chain that had cost me £1,300. They also found £500 in cash on me and knew that a seventeen-year-old probably wasn't making money like that legally. They searched my house and couldn't find anything but my mum told them I often went to the garden shed so they looked there and found my stash of drugs. That was the first time I got arrested and I was released on bail, but managed to get myself arrested again about five or six times that summer for similar stuff.

I nicked a replica gun from a friend and I used to take it to college with me after the summer. I don't even really know why, maybe because I thought it made me look hard. I started getting in more fights and got suspended. Then when there was a massive fight with another gang, someone asked me where my gun was. The conversation was overheard and even though it wasn't a real gun they were referring to, I got expelled from the college.

I got good enough grades to get into uni though and even though I wasn't interested my mum pushed me into it. I met a guy called Danny and he had a similar background to me and we got a place with two other guys, George and Iain. Just a couple of days after starting I was approached by this guy who had stolen £20,000 worth of clothes from a Selfridges truck who wanted to know if I would buy any of it. I spoke to Danny and we agreed we'd rob the guy and get the stuff to sell ourselves. We didn't have much of a plan. We bought

Activities at XLP's COACH weekend away

Young people and leaders from XLP Summer Camp 2009 in Dorset

Collie Smith Drive, Jamaica. This drive used to divide the community in two but now each side is divided into different blocks marking different gang territory. One gang cannot travel into another section.

Bullet Alley, Jamaica. Bullet holes on the side of a house

This car has been overturned to stop drive-by shootings

Patrick and Principal Miss Lorna Stanley of Operation Restoration Secondary School, Jamaica.

Students at Operation Restoration School – 90 per cent of these children do not have a father.

In Jamaica, trainers hanging over a telephone wire mark a death.

Gangs use symbols to mark their territory in LA.

A mural in deprived downtown LA has the names of murdered gang members across the top. Painted in the early 1990s, the mural was an attempt to stop the deaths. The area is home to one of LA's largest and most notorious gangs, '18th Street' who have an estimated 10,000 affiliates and members.

A playground in LA with four exit points – one leading to the territory of each gang in the area.

Patrick Regan and GreenJade before a Gunz Down show

GreenJade performing at
a Gunz Down show

A student at Warren Comprehensive School, Essex shows how The Prince's Trust xl programme has helped him to develop.

The Prince's Trust Team programme members carry out a one-to-one session during their Community Project on a farm in Stratford, East London.

Andy Smith, founder of
Regenerate, Roehampton

Andy Smith and the Regenerate mentoring group after climbing a mountain in Norway.

Students of the Robert Levy Foundation on a day visit to Brands Hatch race circuit as guests of team Motorbase Airways. Here, two students stand with a team driver.

Participants of the Robert Levy Foundation Summer Motor Vehicle Training Programme.

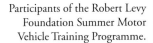

The project for summer 2009 was to build a kit car. These students are receiving their certificates at the end of the course.

stockings for our faces and arranged for Iain to come down too to drive for us. I had a gun that I'd stolen from a friend and I threatened the guy we were getting the goods from. He didn't seem all that surprised; he just put his hands up and got out of the van.

A woman saw us from her window as we were trying to load the gear into the car and she called the police. We tried to outsmart them but they caught Iain and he'd given the police our names and details before they even asked him anything. We were remanded for armed robbery. It was weird hearing that read out in court; it sounded so much more serious than how our actions had seemed to me. All the things we'd got up to just felt normal to me. When it's around you all the time, that's what you know and that's what becomes the norm. I hadn't even thought too much about pointing a gun at that guy and I'd definitely not thought about it as armed robbery. All I'd been thinking about was the money I'd be making.

My dad felt guilty that I'd gone off the rails so he came back for my trial. It was one of only three times I could remember seeing him in my whole life. I wasn't angry with him though – it didn't really bother me whether he was there or not.

The people we stole from wouldn't come to court because obviously they'd stolen the stuff themselves but I was convicted and given a sentence of six years and two months. I didn't feel particularly sorry for the victims but I understood and accepted my punishment and took it on the chin. My barrister's advice was to 'bite the bullet'. That was the first time I ever heard that saying and it stuck with me. It didn't really bother me and the first prison I went to was OK, it was when I went to the second one that was like this huge castle that it hit me and I cried.

I've always been very calculating and too clever for my own good. It's strange 'cos I think if I had channelled these characteristics in a positive manner, they would have been very beneficial. As it is all the events in my life pointed me towards crime.

GUNZ DOWN

Nathaniel's story shows how things can escalate. Tragic situations cause anger and if it is not dealt with, the knock-on effect on someone's life can be huge. Many young people make small decisions like Nathaniel did, getting involved with a group, stealing phones, selling drugs, owning a knife. It starts small but ends up changing their entire future – leading to a life of crime, prison sentences, murder or death. Often young people see things in the very short term. They see a need (for money), they see a solution (robbing someone). They see a problem (someone has disrespected them), they see a solution (beating, stabbing or shooting that person). They do not think through the consequences.

Gunz Down is a programme that XLP started taking into school assemblies in 2006. We feel it meets the vital need to try to get the kids to understand where their actions could lead. One of the things we encourage as part of the show is that problems can be resolved through talking down a situation instead of fighting and using weapons. It may sound simplistic, but actually young people are often not taught to express themselves verbally. Someone makes a comment, or looks at another person in a funny way, or steps on their trainer: they get heated up, they cannot diffuse it themselves, and ultimately the situation escalates to the point where someone is stabbed or shot over nothing.

We aim to grab the kids' attention through hip hop band GreenJade's performances of songs like 'Gunz Down'. They get the whole place going mad as well as delivering positive messages, and then we have some fun with games like challenging Wiz from GreenJade to rap about random objects the kids bring up. When the pupils are all really engaged, I do a section on making choices. The message we are all desperate to get across is that everyone has a choice. As teenagers, in the midst of so much peer pressure and in a culture where violence is becoming the norm, we want to make sure they know that they do not have to do anything. The emphasis is on not rushing decisions and making life-changing choices in the blink of an eye; on not being pushed into decisions because of what anyone else says or does; and on being sussed, i.e. thinking through the consequences of each choice. We use drama as well, with two of the members of GreenJade acting out a scenario of how something small, like someone owing you some money, can escalate into a bigger situation through small choices. Although the tour is called *Gunz Down* and the emphasis is on guns, the same judgements and decision-making processes are relevant whether young people carry knives, get their bull terrier to attack someone, use their fists to make a point, or make any other life choices. We want to make sure it has a broad appeal.

Giving an opportunity for the young people to talk, as well as to listen, at the *Gunz Down* show has been vital. We offer to follow up the hour-long assembly with a series of workshops looking at anger management, how to handle conflict, respect and responsibility. This is done in class groups so they can talk about the issues that impact their decisions regarding guns and knives, such as peer pressure and family environment, in more detail.

The aim of the *Gunz Down* programme is to achieve real transformation of hearts and minds concerning issues of violence, crime and weapons. Our hope is that by exposing the dark reality of making bad choices, we can inform the young people that there are good life choices to be made and that it is worth being courageous. We know it is hard for them to stand up against their friends and peers, but we intend to empower them to choose and give them access to materials that will help them and inspire them to assess their potential actions. We have seen time and time again that wrong choices lead to more wrong choices, which eventually lead to people being defined by those choices: choose violence and murder and you will be defined as a violent murderer. What we want to help people see is that right choices allow them a freedom to choose their own path through life, to explore opportunities and relationships, and to aspire to be like their heroes.

SHARLENE'S STORY

You may remember the words written by Sharlene and her friend Rachel that I quoted at the start of chapter 1. The girls performed at one of our Arts Showcases, which are designed to give young people a chance to display their skills in the performing arts, and their performance was so powerful that we asked them to become a regular part of our *Gunz Down* show. Sharlene took us up on our offer and performs a piece which is based on the death of fifteen-year-old Michael Dosunmu, who attended her school.

Sharlene grew up on an estate where there has historically been a lot of violence. She always stayed away from the gangs, trying to keep her head down and get on with her life. She says she needed to know enough to keep herself safe, but never wanted to get too involved. As someone who sees gang violence going on all around her, she is frustrated and angry about the choices made by some of her peers, believing they are all part of a stupid war that will not get them anywhere. The violence came closer to home when Michael was killed. He was the year below Sharlene at school and the friend of a friend. She vividly recalls the day the year group were told about his death – seeing people filtering away from the hall crying their eyes out. Michael had not been involved in any violence himself; his murder was a case of mistaken identity. Naturally Sharlene was incredibly angry about the situation, but rather than turning to violence herself and following some of the others who were making plans for revenge, she tried to address the problem from a different angle. She put herself in the shoes of Michael's sister, imagining how senseless the loss of her brother was, how much pain she would be in. All because of a crazy postcode war. The Arts Showcase gave Sharlene an opportunity to talk to her peers, to express her frustration at their culture and lifestyles in a way that would make them listen. Having her as part of *Gunz Down* is so powerful – you can see on the audience's faces the impact of her words as she describes the futility of the pain and death that is becoming increasingly common. As she says, 'If just one person hears me and decides not to do something stupid themselves, then it's worth it.'

Sharlene is one of those young people who has faced challenges that lead many into a gang lifestyle, but she has chosen not to get involved. Her parents split up when she was young and she has half-brothers and sisters on both sides, some of whom live with her, some of whom live further away. Like many others, she is frustrated about her lack of money, but has chosen not to make someone else's life miserable in order to enrich her own. When people have threatened her, she has stood up to them, not allowing them to bully her or scare her. She is passionate about the fact that everyone has some talent or gift they can put to good use, that everyone has something to give.

VOICELESS

Many of the people I have spoken to have said that much of their anger comes from feeling that no one wants to listen to them. The government may come up with anti-knife and gun crime legislation, but for the young people themselves it does nothing to address the issue of why they feel the need to carry weapons.

At XLP we are also working on doing an Urban Talk Show to

give more young people like Sharlene a chance to articulate what is happening in their community and in their lives using the performing arts. To try to understand what is going on, politicians have put young people round a table in Westminster to ask them questions, but they find they get very little response. This is not an environment that is comfortable for the average person, let alone someone who is facing some of the struggles we have been talking about. On the other hand, if you get them to rap, sing, write their own poetry or perform a piece of drama, you will be amazed at the insightful stuff that comes pouring out.

We want the Urban Talk Show to be an opportunity for young people to perform different pieces describing what it is like to grow up on an estate, what they want to see happen and how they want to change things. We want to give them a voice, a chance to be heard and ways to express themselves without resorting to violence. In the audience we want politicians, policemen and women, business people – anyone who can make a difference and wants to understand what is going on behind the headlines. There would be opportunities for the young people to have their say through performance as well as a chance for the audience to ask questions to get a better understanding of the current state of affairs. This will be done in conjunction with a mentoring programme like COACH. We have to find ways that allow young people to have a voice in front of those who can do something about their problems. If we put them round a table in Westminster and sit opposite them in suits and ties, they will clam up and shut down – it is too far removed from their world. If the government spend thousands of pounds on ad campaigns telling people not to carry knives, it is not going to make them feel any safer on their streets. They have to be given the chance to express themselves in a way that works for them. And we have to be prepared not only to listen, but also to act, to help in any way we can.

'LIFE IN LYRICS', BY MOHAMMED

Mohammed never got on well with the education system. He moved from school to school to a Pupil Referral Unit, until he quit education. Parental break-up, family in prison and an agoraphobic brother have all featured in his life. Mohammed has been emcee-ing since the age of eight, and he feels he can express himself best in lyrics:

> My life's hardly been sweet
> It's been miserable
> The pain they left inside of me
> Yeah I find mystical
> Mentally and physical
> But slowly turned mythical
> I got so many more lessons to learn
> Just like I was in school
>
> Back then I was too young to understand
> Crossing roads without holding my mum's hand
> And my night turned cold when she weren't around
> And so my mind turned blank
> Like an empty playground
> Sometimes I think to myself 'what am I worth?'
> And 'where do I stand on this cold earth?'
> My life is now all right but it started as a mess
> I just need to find a time to get this pain off my chest.

DANIEL'S STORY

I never really thought of myself as being in a gang. I didn't like the word. To me it was just a group of us who had grown up together, we had each other's backs, went everywhere together. It was all that we knew. Drugs. Knives. Girls. Broken families. It was all around us, but we'd never seen anything different.

I was a pretty angry kid. I was a deep thinker and always had a lot on my mind. I grew up on an estate in Peckham with my mum, dad, one brother and two sisters. My dad left for good when I was fourteen and although I loved him, it was a relief when he left. I couldn't handle how he treated my mum. I grew up around my uncle who was a well-known character in Peckham and Brixton as he used to deal drugs. He and my dad were feared and so people knew who I was by association. My brother is two years older than me and we always hung around together. We were one of the oldest sets of the grandkids in the family so there weren't many big cousins or brothers to defend us and we had to look after ourselves. We wanted to be able to defend ourselves, so when I was seven we took up boxing, aspiring to be like Mike Tyson. The area we lived in was rough and people who didn't live there were sometimes too scared to walk through it. You couldn't find a milkman or a pizza guy who was willing to deliver on the estate. Street fights were the norm. Back then hardly anyone had guns, so if you wanted to protect yourself you had to learn how to fight. People sold and used drugs all over the estate, we'd walk past addicts outside our homes all the time and it made me realise I never wanted to take crack or heroin.

Most of the kids who dropped out of school early started to deal. Their mothers, most of them being single, needed help with the rent and they couldn't get jobs, so selling drugs was the easiest way for them to get money to fend for themselves, putting less strain on their mums.

There was a close network of friends on our estate as we all grew up together and some of us went to the same school. We had really similar experiences of family life, seeing our parents struggling financially, witnessing domestic violence, seeing our families split up. We were all full of anger at what we'd seen and felt hopeless: what could we do about any of it? It tore me up knowing that I couldn't defend my mum from my dad, so much so that it still affects me today. If anyone tried anything on with me, they got the full force of my anger. I started going out raving, and smoking weed helped get things off my mind. I'd been doing pretty well at football, but I dropped out and ended up hanging out more with the other guys who'd all had similar experiences to me growing up. We were going through the same things, so we could talk to each other. I really valued our sense of community.

It also made me angry seeing my mum struggle to pay the bills and buy food for us each week, but I was too young to help. When I was fifteen I managed to get a Saturday job at a local printers earning £20 a week. I figured if I did that and sold some weed, then I wouldn't need to ask my mum for any money, meaning she could use what she earned to buy the food. I wanted to be able to help out, even if it was just giving her £10 every now and then.

PECKHAM VS LEWISHAM

We grew up with a feud between Peckham and Lewisham and everyone was automatically drawn into it, whether they wanted to be or not. Even if you had nothing to do with the Peckham Boys, you had to be aware of Lewisham's Ghetto Boys, and if they came round our way we knew we were going to have to defend ourselves. It pushes you into cliques – us against them. I've known of many cases where guys have been seriously stabbed for being in Lewisham at the wrong time, even though they had no affiliation with the area. Everyone else saw us as the Peckham Boys, even though we knew there were loads of different groups of guys within Peckham not connected to that gang. But it helped when we went out raving that we were all seen as one, as it made us feel safe. Some of the older guys liked me and my brother and when we were out they'd say, 'If anything happens we're over here,' which made us feel safe. We also knew that when other guys saw us with the older lads, they wouldn't start any trouble because they didn't want to start beef with the older guys. We wore similar clothes – the fashion at that time was crisp white trainers with straight jeans and maybe a name-brand top.

My mum and dad taught us strict morals, but those morals clashed with what we saw on the street. They brought me up to know that I was responsible for my actions and one thing I knew I'd never do was steal. My parents are Jamaican, and for them it is a real disgrace on your family if you're a thief. So when my mates were robbing shops to get the latest designer clothes, I never joined in. I stuck to some of the morals my parents taught me, but when I was on the street with my guys I started thinking I was a bad man. I thought, 'No one can do nothing to me.' I guess the street got to my head.

At around seventeen years old I had an encounter with a local crack addict. He attacked my cousin, asking him for money to buy more drugs. We ended up battering him in front of my block, leaving him unconscious. I later found out he was in hospital fighting for his life as he had a clot on his brain, but fortunately he survived. At that point I realised I had come close to killing someone, but that didn't faze me at all. I felt he deserved what he got and I probably would have dealt with him again if he ever approached me.

Because of my boxing training I was good in fights and was known to overcome many in punch-ups. I preferred using my fist rather than using weapons, as I enjoyed the tussle. Every time I won a fight it would enhance my reputation that bit more. People would say, 'This man can rock,' and I'd feel proud. I fought guys from Peckham and Brixton, but I didn't get into any encounters with anyone from Lewisham. I wasn't the type of guy who would look for trouble, but I'd defend my turf. Most fights happened for no real reason at all and at first if you won you'd know you'd got one up on someone and that felt good. But when you've done it so many times, it becomes the norm and you lose any sense of fear, so you'll go into any fight. That's what kids are finding now with guns. Once they've bust a couple of shots, it becomes nothing to pick up a gun and fire it again. The first time might shake them up a bit, but then they get used to it. It's like riding a bike – once you've done it, it's nothing.

Guns are so accessible now, which they weren't in my time. When I was about eighteen, that's when I first held a gun. It was my cousin's and it was a big deal, as guns were really hard to get hold of. He showed me how to load bullets, how to clean it. It was a massive boost for him having it. He wasn't looking to use it, but if he got in a fight and someone was threatening his life, he would have taken them out.

WILL ANYTHING EVER CHANGE?

I used to hang out with a friend on the fifth floor of his block, which looked out over Burgess Park, in Peckham. We'd sit looking at the City buildings, smoking a spliff and thinking about the guys over the river working in the big, posh buildings, living the good life. They had money and we had nothing. They didn't see the struggles we had. We felt like we had no hope. I had no ideas about what I wanted to do as a career. I was studying music technology, but my grades weren't that good and I just didn't know where to go or what to do. Some of my mates just got on benefits, seeing it as free money. Add to that their drugs money and they were nice for the month. For me and many others this felt like a trap, because the moment you tried to move on in life and get a job, you had to pay full rent and more, which then put you in a worse state than when you were on benefits. This didn't make sense to us and made us feel that the government wanted to keep us down and dependent on them. That's why so many people don't care and get involved in drugs and other crime; they would rather make money their way than be a part of a messed-up system. For others the problem was their criminal record. It's so hard to get a job once you've been convicted of anything and it leads to so much frustration and a feeling of helplessness. Even if the offence was ten years ago, it can still put up a barrier, so for lots of people it feels like a life sentence – something they'll never get away from.

I started working part-time at the printers where I'd been doing my Saturday job. I didn't earn much, but it was enough to save up and buy new trainers and go out with my mates, which was all I really wanted. I'd never been on holiday, never travelled anywhere except Buckinghamshire to see family. I was seeing the same things year after year – gang wars, people dying, it was the same old story.

I couldn't help but wonder: would anything ever happen for me? Was life ever going to change?

It was a year later when the killer blow came for me. I went to a rave with some mates and a fight broke out. We got separated in the scuffle, but minutes later a friend got a phone call to say a close friend of ours had been stabbed. I ran to where he was and found him shaking on the floor. I held his hand and looked in his eyes. I kept saying, 'It'll be all right,' over and over again, but I could feel his grip on my hand getting looser and looser.

When we got to the hospital a policeman asked us what had happened, but due to the many bad experiences we'd had with the police, we wouldn't talk. Then he said something that chilled my bones: 'We really need you to talk to us because this could be a murder investigation.' I couldn't believe what I was hearing. Even when I saw my friend on the floor bleeding, I'd never thought he was going to die. 'What did you say?' I managed to ask. 'Is my friend dead?' The policeman told us he couldn't say, but thirty seconds later I got my answer. My friend's mum and dad walked in and as the doctor spoke to them, I heard the loudest scream I've ever heard in my life: that's when I knew he was gone.

My whole world fell apart. I knew I couldn't live a life like that any more. I shut myself away from everything. I left college because I couldn't focus on my music technology course and I didn't do anything except my part-time job. I'd work, go home and sit in my room thinking. At night I'd sometimes walk through the park, thinking about things like whether God was real. I'd been brought up to believe there is a God and it had always stuck with me. We weren't a religious family, but my mum always told me we must give thanks for our food and say our prayers before going to sleep at night. One day, in desperation, I said to God, 'If you're really real, then show yourself to me, 'cos I need you.' I felt so alone, so desperate. I had thoughts of me being the next one to die.

About six months later, a friend asked me to be godfather to his son. I went along to the church service and everything the pastor said seemed to relate to me and my life and was just what I needed. He spoke of a person in desperation, needing answers; it felt to me like that was God's response to my prayer and I knew it was what I'd asked for and what I needed. From that day on, it was a whole fresh start for me.

Of course it was also the beginning of a whole new battle. I'd seen a few people before who'd tried to be humble and move on, get away from the street lifestyle. But there were guys who would see what they were trying to do and would attack them. They'd defend themselves and fight back and then just go back to the old way of life. They felt like they'd tried, but it had only brought them more trouble, so what was the point?

For me the hardest thing was that I still wanted to be around my friends, but I didn't want to be part of the lifestyle any more. I still had to deal with my everyday life, with all the friends who knew me as I had been before. Not long after I committed my life to God, a group of us were at my house when one of them got a phone call. Some beef kicked off with another group of guys who were round the corner from my house. I used to keep planks of wood and other homemade stuff under my wardrobe to be used as weapons and hadn't got rid of them yet, so everyone started picking them up and saying, 'Let's go.' I took hold of one, but inside all I could think was that I didn't want to do this any more. I was in the process of changing, but the change couldn't keep pace with the situations I was dealing with. As I went through my bedroom door, following my friends out to this fight, I fell to my knees. 'Help me, God,' I prayed. 'I don't want to live like this any more, but I've got to go out and back my friends.' I got up, but to my surprise everyone was walking back towards my flat. 'This is weird,' I thought. 'What happened?' I asked. 'They're gone,' came the reply. No one else understood why they'd left – no one ever backed out of a fight. But I believed that my prayer made all the difference and God was trying to help me find a way out.

My friends didn't really get my new belief in God and some of them didn't know how to take it. A lot of them stopped coming to see me, I think because they just didn't understand. Everyone was dealing with the death of our friend in their own way and they couldn't all relate to me. I began to question these friendships. I stopped smoking in my house and then even fewer people came to see me, so I was left wondering: were my friendships built on sitting round smoking together? Was that it? I was questioning every aspect of my life.

I wanted to try new things, so I left my job at the printers. The manager there, Mrs Rose, backed me up completely. She was like family to me, accepting who I was and who I wanted to become, supporting me as I tried to work out what I wanted to do next. I went to work in a bank and, to be honest, I didn't enjoy it, as I felt it was boring just sitting there giving and taking money. I wanted to do more, but at least it was experience. I stayed there for about seven months and during that time I got chatting to lots of people. All my life it seemed it had just been about me and my boys, now I was speaking to a lot more older people and I realised I could learn a lot from them. I had no role models to look up to. I hadn't even realised till then that no one older had ever helped me learn from their experiences. I started to crave more and spent hours talking to different people from church, some of my mum's friends and people at the printers. It gave me a whole new outlook on life. Even when I walked into a food shop I'd start talking to people behind the till – whoever I came across I'd make time to say more than just hello. I wanted to find out where they were coming from and see what their life was like.

When I left the bank I spent a gap year with a youth organisation.

It was another turning point for me and I found myself being able to share my story and talk about my experiences with other young people who were going through similar things. They'd grown up all over the country, but our stories were similar in many ways.

We got on the train to go to York on a residential course and I couldn't help but stare out of the window, looking at all the cows and sheep! It may sound funny, but you don't get that type of scenery where I'm from. When we got there I was the only black guy in the room. That had never happened to me before. I didn't know where people were coming from in terms of their life experiences, but as they shared their stories and struggles I began to think that maybe Peckham wasn't such a bad place to grow up. I realised things could have been a lot worse. The course gave me a whole new outlook on life. I wanted to seek out every opportunity I could to experience something new and different. We began working in schools, setting up our own projects, and for the first time I felt a sense of ownership in something. I was suddenly aware that I had potential; I could do something with my life.

The most important thing was that I began to feel like a whole new person. I had a new identity. I wasn't this rude boy or street boy any more. I was Daniel – a person who could achieve whatever I set out to achieve. What I most wanted to do was share what I had learned with other guys like me and like the mates I had grown up with. I wanted to give advice to those guys who didn't have someone to look up to.

During this time of change I began a new relationship. I'd known Olivia for many years, as we'd met at a mutual friend's house earlier, but we began to see each other more closely. A few years later we were married, which was such a major thing for both us and our families, as marriages don't happen often in our community. My wife has always been a great support to me. She grew up in the church, which gave her a very different approach to life from me, even though she'd shared some of the same experiences that I had. My wife has helped me to aim high and reach beyond what I think I can achieve. She is a rock in my life.

I even have a great relationship with my dad now. He was man enough to apologise for the wrongs he did. I've never been so close to him before.

Now I work for another youth charity doing detached youth work. I never thought I'd find a job that suited me so well. It seems to involve all of my personal interests like music, mentoring, speaking to young people and working with different types of media. It's incredible to have a platform to develop my personal skills and reach out to young people, and it's a privilege to be a role model for guys who are dealing with situations like those I faced when I was younger. It really hit home how needed this work is with one particular boy I was working with in a school. He'd been dealing with some really tough issues and one day a colleague of mine found him sleeping rough on the streets. His mum had kicked him out and he had nowhere to go. My colleague saw my phone number written on his hand. He didn't have any money to contact me, but it was me he wanted to speak to. He was willing to open up to me and trusted me; it was amazing to be able to be there for him when he felt that even his family had given up on him. It's incredible to me that I've gone from being someone who didn't really have much hope for my own future, to being in a position where I can impact the lives of other young people in a really positive way and help them overcome some of the obstacles in their lives.

9

The Role of the Media

I've seen news crews attending scenes of shootings with
no regard for the community or the tragedy that had just
occurred. I remember one kid being told to f*** off in the
street by a cameraman, despite the fact that it was one
of his friends that was lying in critical condition in the
hospital.

(*Chris Macintosh, youthworker, Manchester*)

At XLP we get phone calls from the media fairly regularly. Usually
they want to follow a gang leader for a day, speak to young guys
carrying weapons and get details on violent acts that have been
carried out, like gang rape. My response is always the same: I know
young people who are carrying knives and are in gangs, but I know
more who are not doing those things, even though they struggle
with the same issues as other teenagers. I always say to the journal-
ist, 'Why don't you talk to them about why they've chosen *not* to
do those things? Give them an opportunity to become role models
for others in their community.' To date, no one has ever taken me
up on this offer.

We all know how it works: to sell papers, headlines have to be
sensational. Some papers have started 'death toll counters' on their
front pages, referring to the number of teenagers who have lost
their lives to gangs and knife or gun crime. My fear is that when

we start to see headline numbers we lose any sense that we are talking about real people, real lives. People become statistics, another death to add to the grand total, rather than a life wiped out, a family and community devastated by the senseless loss. Other papers go with headlines like 'Crime Britain', 'Gang Fear Grips Capital', 'Toll Of Stabbed Children Doubles'. These sorts of phrases regularly scream from news stands and if you just give them a quick glance, you would think that all our youth are running wild, drugged up and crime crazed. The truth is far from that: gang involvement is still a minority activity and the newspapers who print these headlines should be held responsible for the fact that they are essentially scaremongering. Our media are helping to breed a culture of fear and so society becomes more afraid of young people, leaving them further isolated. Who wants to get involved and go and help teenagers if they think they will be stabbed for their efforts? For the young people themselves, the headlines do not help either. They are constantly being told that everyone else is carrying a weapon, so they start to think they need one too, either to use as a form of self-defence or just in order to be like everyone else.

There is even an argument that some gangs commit violent acts to get their fifteen minutes of fame. While lots of gang members shy away from the media, wanting to keep their activities hidden, others have recently shown a willingness to be seen on TV and in the press holding weapons and looking defiant. Why? As a further way to establish that they do not care about authority, that no one can get to them, and to try to gain more respect for themselves and their gang. To that end, it is not hard to imagine that in such a context many of the guys would exaggerate what they and their gang get up to – they embellish stories to create fear in other gangs and make themselves look hard. Research done in Chicago showed that one group, whom the police called the 'Whatever Boys', ended up in the newspapers for their actions. Once they had experienced their first taste of being in the media, all they did was work to get back into the papers.[1]

In general the papers deny that they influence culture, maintaining that all they do is reflect it. I met with an editor of one of the red tops a number of years ago and he got extremely defensive when I asked if the negative stories his paper printed created a culture of fear and worsened the problems. The issue is that the average person in the UK has to work out the actual reality of the situations splashed all over the press. We all know not to believe everything we read, yet I would guess that the majority of us do believe a lot of what the papers tell us. It is vital that we paint a picture of what life is really like for thousands of teenagers in our country today, instead of grabbing people's attention with the most horrific stories. Wouldn't it be wonderful if we could give credit to the young people who are making positive choices? Their stories may not be as hard hitting, but they might help other young people in difficult situations to find hope and the tools to change their lives and turn things around before it is too late.

DOCUMENTARIES

There is a growing trend for television documentaries featuring the issue of gang culture in Britain's inner cities. This is great for raising awareness, but a nightmare if only one side of the story is shown. Take Ann Widdecombe's 2007 television documentary for ITV about the Andover Estate in London, where she went to report on anti-social behaviour. She talked to older residents who said they were living in fear of the young people on the estate, detailing vandalism, beatings, excrement left outside front doors and the fear of leaving their homes. While these are certainly frightening stories, the local council and the young people from the estate said the reports were exaggerated and the interviews only represented one side of the estate. In fact, the young people were so outraged at the inaccurate portrayal of their area that they produced their own video in response. Their video highlighted some of the positives – young people persevering and trying to make life work, and a community of friends who have grown up together. Those residents felt completely misrepresented by Ann Widdecombe's programme. Can you imagine how it feels when you are trying really hard to overcome some pretty difficult circumstances, and then you are judged by someone from an entirely different socio-economic background? Many on the Andover Estate said the damage was pretty far reaching and there were reports that some of the young people were beaten up by kids from other estates because they were made to look weak by the programme.

When the media report on estates or about young people, they are in a position to do something positive and help instead of stereotyping the groups and isolating them even further. So many people watch these programmes and accept what they are shown as fact. In the case of the Widdecombe programme, existing negative stereotypes of young people were merely reinforced. As one of the girls from the estate said, 'It makes me feel frustrated, 'cos the media and older generation may think that all we do is harass people and sell drugs.'

We must remember when we talk about these issues that we are talking about areas and estates that are people's homes. Most of us have some sense of loyalty to places where we have grown up or lived for a long time. We may be aware of the challenges and the problems, but we will probably still have a strong attachment to our home. That is no different if you have grown up on an estate.

As the Widdecombe programme showed, people are offended when they feel that the issues they are facing are misrepresented and the virtues of their community are ignored.

SOCIAL MEDIA

The rapid rise in the ownership of mobile phones has had a huge impact on the ability of gangs to organise fights. What might have once taken days, even weeks, to set up can kick off in a matter of minutes with chains of people sending texts or making phone calls to get everyone in one place for a fight. The sophistication of the technology has changed things too. By carrying a mobile phone, young people are able to video and photograph anything at a moment's notice and send those images on to other friends within seconds. When you hear about groups of young people committing violent attacks, you will often hear that at least one member of the gang was recording the events on their mobile phone. As well as being passed from mobile to mobile, these videos are often uploaded to websites like YouTube and networking sites like Facebook and MySpace for hundreds of others to see. It is another way for gangs to boast about their exploits, to create fear and show their power and domination.

The rise in TV music channels can also be said to play a part in the frustrations and aggression in young men as well. Programmes like *Cribs* show stars like 50 Cent walking round their huge mansions, with their fleet of cars lined up on the drive. Kids look at that and they think, 'I want that kind of lifestyle. I've got to find some way to get it.' Other stations give an opportunity for anyone to submit music videos to be aired, so you get gangs rapping about what they are going to do to other gangs on TV.

INFLUENCE OF MUSIC

The impact of music in terms of stimulating violence in young people has long been debated. Most people would agree that music alone does not cause someone to become aggressive. After all, kids all over the place listen to albums from artists like 50 Cent and remain peaceful; they can enjoy the music even without being able to relate to the lyrics. However, when that same music is heard by a young person who has been excluded from school, someone who sees no hope for their future and is surrounded by violence, the words take on a whole new meaning. That young person is much more likely to put into practice the lyrics relating to sex and violence, much more likely to relate to a lifestyle where a gun seems a necessary accessory. Music can stimulate feelings of aggression and rage; the words may seem to express how they are feeling and their frustrations with life. The music may be the same, but the responses of two different children from two different areas and backgrounds can be polar opposites.

John Sutherland, Superintendent of Islington Borough Police, agrees that music may not be the cause, but it is providing an unhelpful influence: 'If you take the violence that is apparent in some rap music, if you combine that with violence apparent in an awful lot of video games, feature films and horror porn, combine that with material available on the internet, if you take any of those, either in isolation or together: do I think they are to blame? No. Do I think they help or hinder? I think they profoundly hinder.'

I also spoke to Wizdom from hip hop group GreenJade about the influence of music and whether he thinks it can lead to violence. He told me, 'No one song, video game or film can make a person violent, promiscuous or suicidal. However, if you consume a lot of it, it creates an environment where those things are possible because the mind begins to accept them as a result of the messages it is fed. I grew up listening to hip hop heavily from about the age of eleven and immersed myself in that world and music. I used to swear like a sailor working on a building site, but when I immersed myself in an environment where people did not swear and it was unacceptable, I stopped. A horrifying statistic is that 63 per cent of offenders' children offend, mainly because they have grown up in an environment where that is acceptable. To really make an impact we need to affect the environment a person is in.'

Melvyn Davis, founder and director of The Male Development Service (BoyztoMEN), summed it all up by saying:

The evidence across the board is that more white people buy hardcore rap, but you don't see them going off shooting and stabbing and killing each other. Because it's translated differently. It's internalised differently . . . the ones on whom it impacts most, and it has the most influence, are the ones coming from that demographic where there's an absent father, they don't have very much going on themselves, school's not working. And they have very limited life experiences which means for them, what they see on the TV, that's real. What they experience via the music becomes their reality. Because they don't have a wider experience or a deeper experience, they can't displace that and say 'That's just music.'[2]

I completely agree that music can create an atmosphere and an environment where all sorts of things are acceptable. Rap lyrics seem to know no boundaries when it comes to sex, killing people, prison, stealing, drugs – it is all there. Anecdotal evidence suggests that some listen to this kind of music to pump themselves up before a fight, saying it helps them 'get in the zone' for what they are about to do.

A POSITIVE INFLUENCE

The media holds so much power in our society and when they use that power for the good of the community, it can do amazing things. Take the Pride of Britain Awards as an example of a national newspaper (the *Mirror*) honouring people who give themselves tirelessly to others in their communities. I know our local South London Press do something similar and I am sure many other media outlets try to find ways to reward and acknowledge some of the amazing people in our country. Entertainment programmes can have a real impact too, like when MTV and EMI worked with XLP on a *Pimp My Ride* special. The show normally does up a run-down car, but we got the police to give us an old police riot van and EMI sponsored MTV to turn it into a mobile recording studio for young people. Not only did it benefit loads of the young people we work with, but the programme was also seen by thousands of others and through speaking to some young people, it gave a national platform to some of the issues they are facing. MTV and EMI were also brilliant in offering ongoing support and getting artists to come down and do workshops with anyone who wanted to take part.

There are so many opportunities for those who work in the media to use their influence to raise awareness of issues and to use their reach to help others. Whether it is the dramatisation of real issues like the ITV programme about the hunt for Jamie Robe's killers, or websites like TrueTube that encourage communities to make and post videos that give voice to the things they are facing, there is so much scope for us to use the media to give young people a chance to make their voice heard and for us all to get a better picture of what is really going on across our country.

Part Three

Where Do We Go From Here?

10

Taking Action

We are called to play the Good Samaritan on life's
roadside, but that will be only an initial act. One day
we must come to see that the whole Jericho Road must
be transformed so that men and women will not be
constantly beaten and robbed as they make their journey
on life's highway. True compassion is more than flinging
a coin to a beggar. It comes to see that an edifice which
produces beggars needs restructuring.

(*Martin Luther King, Jr*)

I t is a horrifying situation. I have tried not to be sensationalist, but
the facts speak for themselves and you would be forgiven for
thinking that it is hopeless, that nothing can be done. It is true that
there are no quick fixes, no magic wand that will stop this gang
culture in an instant, but there is hope. At the moment we are in a
position where we can – and must – act in order to stop gang
violence from becoming institutionalised across our country. If we
fail, we will see the problem get worse, continue to spread out from
our inner cities into other areas, and future generations will be
devastated by ongoing and worsening violence. So what can we do?

When you start talking about potential solutions, there tend to
be two approaches. One is the 'stick' method, proposing longer
prison sentences, tougher prisons, more stop and search powers for

the police, knife arches in train stations, tougher discipline in schools and forcing parents to take more responsibility for their kids. Some even suggest that reintroducing National Service would quickly change our young people for the better.

The other approach is, of course, the 'carrot', a method favoured by the voluntary sector. The philosophy is concerned with raising aspirations, providing meaningful employment, offering alternatives to gangs, and understanding the effects of persistent poverty and lack of education on children. The bottom line is to create opportunities through understanding the issues.

As for me, I believe the situation is often much more complex than we think (and perhaps you will agree, having read more about some of these issues). As we have seen through some of the people we have talked about in this book, there are complex reasons why people get drawn into gangs. There may be some underlying similarities, but every individual has a different story to tell, a different journey that has led them to that place. Things vary around the country and from city to city. Some are on the periphery of gangs; others are in so deep they would risk their lives for the sake of their fellow gang members. What is certain is that one issue alone does not cause a person to turn to a gang. We will all know people who face some of the issues we have discussed here, like growing up in a single-parent family, dealing with poverty, living in a tough area or not doing well at school; and we know they have not turned to crime, violence and gangs. It is when a number of these factors come together that a young person can be pushed towards such a life.

COMMUNITY-LED SOLUTIONS

There is an old African saying that it takes a village to raise a child. We have a lot to learn from this mentality and it is key if we are to address some of these issues. If we want to impact our communities and see them changed, then we have to be involved in our communities and take ownership of them. Right at the heart of any solution has to be listening to and understanding our community and what they are facing. But this has to be done seriously and followed through. I have seen situations before where MPs will talk to young people in the wake of a gang murder and say they want to understand and listen. The fact is, I have rarely seen any follow-up after that one meeting and so, whatever the MPs intentions were, the act comes across as tokenistic. The worst thing is that it makes the young people who are asked for their opinions feel used by those in power: as far as they can see, the MP was only there to look good and to get a photo opportunity. The young people are left even angrier. What is the point of telling someone about the issues if that person is not going to do anything about them?

This means that in order for any 'solutions' to work, they have to be led by those in the community. That does not mean that if we are not living in that community we should not get involved, but if we are serious about seeing some change, we go in, we ask, we listen and we act on what we are told. A project called 'Regenerate' highlights exactly how this can work in practice. When Andy Smith and some friends wanted to bring hope to the young people on their estate, they started by simply asking what was needed and the project grew in amazing ways from those simple beginnings. More details about Regenerate are given a little later in this chapter.

YOUTH-LED INITIATIVES

Initiatives that are led by the young people themselves are key. At XLP we have just introduced a Youth Volunteer Award, because we wanted to recognise some of the great stuff the young people are doing as well as involving them in our strategies. This award is for people like Steven. As a fast runner, someone like Steven is invaluable to gangs when they are stealing things and so he was recruited. They would grab something like a laptop from a commuter on their way home and Steven would leg it so fast no one stood a chance of catching up with him. If the other guys were caught, they had nothing on them and were in the clear. Steven decided he wanted out when he saw the gang beating up a guy they were stealing from. They punched the victim repeatedly in the face, even as he fell to the floor, and at the age of fourteen, it was too much for Steven. Thankfully he heard that we had MTV and EMI coming to work with us on their *Pimp My Ride* special turning an old police riot van into a mobile recording studio. MTV wanted four young people to be involved in the programme and talk about youth violence in London. Steven auditioned for the show and got chosen. He said that being on TV made people look at him differently and made him realise he could achieve something. Now he comes onto our bus every week as a volunteer, working with other young people and trying to stop them from going down the same route he took. If he had continued with his old life, he would now be in a very different place. He has found a positive way to use his love of sports by coaching football, and he uses his creative talents to design flyers for our events. Likewise with Sharlene, mentioned earlier. Her performance in *Gunz Down* gets a strong reaction from the audience every time because she is a young girl who knows what others of her age are going through. She gives up her time to perform in front of different schools to try to reach young people and help them make better choices. We want to recognise and reward young people like Steven and Sharlene who are giving their time to help others.

ACCESSIBLE ROLE MODELS

To give young people an idea of what they can achieve, we need to be highlighting good role models. I am not talking about people who have become rich and famous, but about those who have lived with (and therefore understand) the issues being faced by teenagers today: those who have overcome challenges and become music teachers, started their own businesses, work on websites or have trained as electricians – anything that shows a positive lifestyle. When we have our Arts Showcases, we try to bring in special guests, people who can show the young people that they can achieve the things they want. There is always an amazing response as our guests stand up and describe their journey and then perform. Sometimes the role models the media hold up are too far removed from the young people we are working with, so to find someone who went to their school or who lived on their estate is very special. We have to hold up these people as well as getting them to be mentors to young people who need some positive role models in their lives.

LANGUAGE

Another part of the challenge for us all is the language we choose to use in connection with these issues. We are often so quick to label and stereotype people and areas, and if we are not careful it all becomes a self-fulfilling prophecy. As we discussed earlier, a lot of our young people are struggling to find any hope for themselves and their future. How does it impact them if we talk about 'feral youth' and a generation of violent criminals with no boundaries? When an MP recently came to film a documentary on an estate in London, he did a piece to camera talking about it being one of the most deprived estates in Europe. I was with him and cut in, asking him how he thought the 7,500 people living there would feel about that. He was baffled: he had never thought about it like that. We have to recognise the positives as well as the reality of the negatives. There may be areas of deprivation, but let us also talk about how many amazing people live there; about how many have faced the challenges of poverty and crime and overcome them.

FUNDRAISING FOR VOLUNTARY SECTOR GROUPS

I will admit up front that this is a bugbear of mine, because it is something that impacts my work every day at XLP, but I know I am not alone in my frustrations. When I started out in youth work, I was going into schools and meeting with kids all the time. I loved it. Now things have grown and XLP has become much more 'successful', if you like, but I spend the majority of my time fundraising just to keep everything going. Many faith-based organisations like ours are treated with suspicion when the truth is that we are not trying to force our beliefs on anyone, we are just motivated by our faith to try to make a difference.

The reality is that many voluntary sector groups live in their communities, so they understand the issues better than anyone and know what is needed. Many are putting their ideas into practice, but are so severely underfunded that much of their time goes into fundraising rather than getting on with the project itself. If you speak to a voluntary sector worker, you are likely to find someone who is passionate and committed but, to be honest, usually exhausted. It is also incredibly disheartening for them that they have to fight for every penny and then the government spends £3 million on an ad campaign against knife crime. Considering the issues I have raised in this book, do you think that seeing a poster will change someone's mind about the knife they are carrying? Does it really get to the heart of the problem or help young people?

Often the 'sexy' projects are the ones that get funding too. Understandably, everyone wants to be involved in high-profile, exciting projects, but there are very few who want to pay for the core costs of running a charity that allow for those sexy projects to happen. The projects that can claim to be working with 'thousands' of young people are far more likely to get funding than those working with individuals one on one in order to get truly effective results.

SPEND $1 AND SAVE $17

Research done in the United States has shown that spending money on intervention and prevention programmes saves a considerable amount of money in the long run. It could be as much as $17 of benefit for every $1 spent, and maybe even much more.[1] This is without trying to factor in the emotional costs to family, friends and communities of the violence and crime. How is it so much? Over time the average person in a gang will run up a huge bill in terms of the following:

- the criminal justice system (with police, courts and prisons);
- local authorities who pick up the costs of gang-related criminal damage;
- the education system (classroom disruption, truancy and exclusion);
- the benefits system if they are out of work;
- HM Revenue & Customs (for lost tax revenue).

To give you an idea of costs, in the UK it takes £164,750 to keep a young person in a Secure Training Unit for one year. The police spend a minimum of £1.1 million investigating every murder. They often spend literally millions of pounds putting together a case against gangs, only to find that people will not talk, there is not enough evidence and the gang walks free. The Home Office estimates that the NHS and Criminal Justice System spend £4 billion annually because of homicide and woundings.[2] If we spent the money upfront on the right things, we could save ourselves not only a lot of money, but a great deal of heartache in the long term.

GREATER COLLABORATION

Those of us who work in the voluntary sector know that there are others out there doing similar work to ours. It takes time and it takes energy, but if we commit to working together, sharing best practice, learning from each other and supporting one another, we will help each other achieve our goals. Also, the more we work with the police, the more we will be able to help. In Los Angeles the police have the numbers of local charities in their phones. If there is a problem and they think the charity can help, they can get in touch there and then. Similarly in Jamaica, church pastors have a large influence on the community, so much so that if fighting breaks out, the pastors are the ones who are called to mediate as they have more power than the police.

Over the years XLP has teamed up with a number of organisations in order to offer the best possible support to communities, because we know that as just one organisation we do not come anywhere close to having all the answers. We have worked with police engagement teams to offer a weekly support group to victims of crime, and with the council's housing department and police crime prevention teams as we have taken our youth centre bus onto the estates. We have found it really beneficial to work with the police, particularly when we put on an Arts Showcase event together, because it helps the young people to see that the police are not just there to stop and search them. We have a number of businesses that support us financially, as well as sending their employees as volunteers to work on our bus in the evenings, which has been fantastic. We have also introduced a City basketball event in the heart of London, where businesses pay to compete against each other and against teams of the young people who live on the estates where we work. This has not only raised vital funds for our work, but has offered an important opportunity for these two groups to interact on the 'level playing field' of a basketball court. The challenge is to keep seeing where aims and objectives of charities and other organisations overlap and looking for opportunities to work together. We are particularly keen to develop long-term relationships with others so that we can put on regular activities and not just one-off events.

SO WHAT CAN WE DO?

If we want to tackle the gang problem effectively, we have to take a number of approaches. We need to help young people who are currently in gangs to find a way out. We need to offer help to those who are in prison or who are coming out and will struggle to find work with their criminal record. We need to work with young people when they have been stabbed or shot and help them find a way of managing their anger, rather than going out and trying to kill someone in retaliation. But we also need to intervene earlier to try to stop young people from ever getting into gangs in the first place.

Over the following pages you will find examples of individuals and groups working to help young people who are vulnerable to some of the different triggers that drive teenagers towards gangs. They are intervening at different times and in different ways, and the stories of success are inspiring.

EARLY INTERVENTION – CHANCE UK

Chance UK do some fantastic work, mentoring children who are between five and eleven years old but already show signs of behavioural difficulties, many of them on the verge of being excluded from school. The weekly one-on-one sessions aim to introduce more stability into each child's life and to give that child someone to talk to at a time when he or she is feeling isolated. The mentor can directly address the difficulties experienced by each child and support that individual as he or she finds the motivation and life skills necessary for moving forward. Through the sessions the mentor can also help channel the child's disruptive energy into projects that encourage a sense of personal achievement and help give the child a sense of self-worth.

Alex is a classic example of a child who can be helped through a mentoring project like Chance UK. He was just a year old when he was left in the care of his grandmother after his mother was sent to prison. His dad was not around consistently, but when he was there, he was providing a worrying example to his child through his own involvement in gangs. By the age of six, Alex's anger was often out of control. His grandmother said his tantrums were uncontrollable and would often last up to an hour. At school he was verbally aggressive and violent towards the other pupils and bullied the more vulnerable kids around him. But of course, despite his outward appearance, Alex was still a vulnerable six-year-old child himself. He was fearful of making mistakes or getting things wrong, and found it hard to confide in others.

Alex's school referred him to Chance UK – seeing that without some one-on-one time with a positive role model, Alex could easily go down the road of gangs and crime later in life. Because of his love of football, Alex requested a sporty mentor and was matched with a man in his late thirties, Bradley. At first Alex was painfully shy with Bradley and displayed both his fierce temper and his extreme fear of failure. Bradley spent time explaining to Alex that his frustrations were understandable, but that he alone was responsible for his actions and he could choose how he responded in different situations. He helped Alex to see that he did not need to destroy his work every time he thought he had made a mistake. He could simply adjust it. Through reinforcing these positive messages and addressing Alex's concerns about himself, Bradley was able to give Alex more confidence in himself.

As well as talking, Bradley and Alex connected over shared interests such as playing football, doing quizzes and drawing dream cars. In addition to their one-on-one time together, Bradley and Alex took part in Chance UK organised outings with other children and their mentors. These involve activities like canal trips, visits to libraries and museums, taking part in workshops, or getting involved in sports or educational games.

Nine months into the mentoring experience, Alex's temper had completely changed. As his grandmother explained, he would still get angry, but only for a minute or two – instead of the hour-long tantrums he was producing before he met Bradley.

Alex is not a one-off example. A study found that by the end of their mentoring year, 98 per cent of children had fewer behavioural difficulties and 51 per cent had no difficulties at all.[3] As for long-term impact, 93 per cent of the children who at the start of their mentoring were deemed at risk of developing anti-social or criminal behaviour in the future had not been in trouble with the police up to five years after the completion of the Chance UK programme.

Working with the parents

Of course, it is not just the children who need support. Chance UK offer the parents and carers of children in the mentoring scheme help through their ParentPlus initiative as well. This means they have someone to talk to about what is happening in their lives, a chance to ask questions about parenting or get practical help with issues such as budgeting or accessing adult education. As well as giving the parents support, this aids better communication between parents and children and improves their relationship in the long run.

Could you be a mentor?

If you have been reading this and thinking you would like to get involved and support a young person, mentoring could be a fantastic place to start. Mentors do not need to have particular skills and qualifications and Chance UK provide mentors with ongoing training and support. Mentors need to be available for two to four hours once a week for a year, and also need to take time to plan their sessions and attend a supervision session once a month at the Chance UK offices. If you would like to make a huge difference in a child's life, why not contact Chance UK to see if you can get involved? See details on their website at www.chanceuk.com/mentor. Chance UK began in London (Hackney, Islington and Lambeth) and because of its success has now rolled out to Liverpool, Hemel Hempstead, Inverness and Derry, and is in more discussions to expand the programme to other areas.

REGENERATE, AN URBAN YOUTH PROJECT

Andy works on the Alton Estate in Roehampton, south-west London, one of the largest housing estates in Europe. I met him a couple of years ago when he invited me to talk to some young people in gangs or on the edge of them about my experiences in Trenchtown. I was impressed by Andy's style of youth work and what he and his team were doing. As you will see from his story, their approach was to ask the community what they needed and how Regenerate could help, and this came from a genuine desire to be part of the solutions to their community's problems.

Andy's story

I first moved onto the Alton Estate with a few friends, just because it was a cheap place to live, but it did not take long before we began to see some of the crazy stuff that was going on in people's lives. We would see ten-year-olds riding stolen mopeds, people being bottled in the pub and others getting stabbed in the street. Teenagers were addicted to drugs and often around the estate there would be the burnt-out remains of stolen cars. We heard of elderly people who had not left their homes for twenty years. It was depressing to see all this stuff being commonplace and we wanted to bring some hope to the area. There was nothing going on for the young or elderly residents and my friends and I started to dream about what we could do to make a difference in the community.

One evening my mum helped me write a proposal for the council to ask for money to start a charity. They gave us a small amount of money to start Regenerate, and so we began running some after-school sessions for young people and a lunch club for the elderly in a rented church building. We employed another youth worker to work alongside me and right at the start we sat down with one of the local kids who was eleven years old and always getting into trouble. We asked him what he would like us to do and he came up with a whole list, starting with playing football and including skiing (although we later found out he meant ice-skating – he just didn't know what it was called!). The following week we put jumpers down on the green as goalposts and started a weekly football club with about ten kids. The week after that, someone donated five-a-side goalposts and our weekly football club has been running ever since, and that was ten years ago. One of my female friends was studying dance at Roehampton University, so she set up a street dance club for the girls. It was so popular that it quickly became two groups, as about sixty or seventy girls wanted to get involved.

The drop-in sessions we ran were pretty simple. They were in the church hall and although we had a table tennis table, we didn't even have a net – we had to use a pile of books for a while! But it wasn't about putting on amazing entertainment, it was just a chance for us to invest in the young people, get to know them and support them when they were having a hard time. We became like big brothers and sisters in many ways and found that the young people opened up to us really easily when they knew we were there for them.

In the holidays we would arrange trips on the back of what the young people had asked for – simple things like swimming or ice-skating or taking a group in the minibus to see the coast. I remember one cold day, as we pulled up to the beach, a twelve-year-old boy jumped out of the minibus and ran into the sea fully clothed. 'What are you doing?' we asked him, thinking he was mad. 'I've never seen the sea,' he said, 'I just wanted to run into it.'

Because we were still running lunches for the elderly, we knew we needed a separate space for the young people. We had no funds, but took a rented shop on the estate that was derelict and hoped the money would come in to do it up. We needed about £20,000 and money started coming through in bits and pieces. I remember at one point we had twenty-four hours to pay the electrician the £3,500 he was owed for his work. A group of young people were knocking on the door asking when we'd be opening. 'When we get the money,' we told them. One of them said, 'Why don't you pray?' So we said, 'Why don't you?' Well, they did, and by the next morning I had received three different cheques that totalled the £3,500 we needed. The Juice Bar opened and became a safe place for the young people to come where they could just hang out, play games, do arts and crafts and have group discussions. We had no official funding (the council were only covering the elderly people's lunch clubs), but we managed to keep going through gifts from local churches and individuals who had heard about what we were doing.

A few years after we started the youth work in Roehampton, some friends of mine told me they were working with street children in Kenya and asked if I wanted to go out there with them. I jumped at the chance to learn from their projects. While we were there, they held a camp for the street kids and asked if we wanted to bring some young people from London back with us for the camp the following year. So the next year we took a group of eight young people from Roehampton out to Africa. One of the lads who came with us was Luke, who was eighteen. I'd known him since he was fourteen, when he would always be mucking about outside Regenerate with a knife, trying to look hard. He'd had a tough start in life. Luke's mum died when he was eight and one night, not long after, someone walked into his home and put a gun to his head. That was the way he found out that his dad was a drug dealer: the gunman threatened to kill Luke if he didn't show him where the drugs and the money were. His dad was in and out of prison, so Luke was shipped around foster carers and, perhaps unsurprisingly, began using drugs regularly when he was just thirteen. Ever since we met him, he was always getting into trouble with the police for petty burglaries and breaking into people's garages, but we built up a good relationship with him and he always got stuck into activities we'd arranged. Luke seemed pretty lost. Although his tutor at school had helped him get an apprenticeship as a mechanic, he was smoking weed every day and we thought he'd really benefit from being in a completely different environment, even for just a couple of weeks.

For Luke, that trip to Kenya was a completely life-changing experience. Although he'd lived in what we would call poverty for most of his life, there in Kenya he saw poverty on a whole different level. There are kids who are all alone, they sleep on the streets, have no shoes, spend their days sniffing glue, can't go to school and get their food from dustbins. But Luke also saw that the people in Kenya had great faith and that inspired him, leading him to become a Christian himself. His new faith made Luke realise he wanted to do something that made a difference in the world and, as he said, be 'a voice for the voiceless'. He overheard Sammy, a guy we were working with in Kenya, talking about the need for employment opportunities in their village and how amazing it would be to have a garage where people could work. A garage would provide an income for lots of families, meaning they could put meals on their tables as well as paying for their kids to go to school. Young guys who previously were living on the streets could get trained up and get a job at the garage too. Straight away Luke said, 'I want to do that. I want to help build that garage.' I didn't realise what a big-scale project it would be and his determination to make it happen has blown me away. When we came back to the UK, Luke started saving hard. Each week he'd come and see me to hand over £100 from his apprenticeship pay, and after six weeks he had enough money to buy a small plot of land in Kenya. Having something to focus on, having a purpose, meant that Luke was able to give up the drugs. It took him three years and lots of fundraising, but he managed to raise £30,000 to get a garage started in Kenya to help the community. He and others from the estate went over to help build it. The garage will employ around thirty-five people and has already employed a number of people to help build it. More than that, it has already done a lot for the area: people have seen that a business is opening up and have bought surrounding pieces of land to build homes on. The garage will also have a training centre and a restaurant – the project just keeps getting bigger and the community are very excited about it. Luke goes over every few months to work there and see everyone and he said, 'Before I went to Kenya I didn't know where I was going in my life – I didn't have no goals or dreams. I was sick of what I was doing; it wasn't helping me. People helped me in my life and it changed me, now I want to do that for other people.'

Luke has really inspired other young people from the estate. If he can do something, then *they* can do something. A few of the young people who have been heavily involved in gang life and street violence have decided that they too want to make a difference. When we first moved onto the estate, though there were a lot of young people getting into trouble, there weren't gangs as such. Now gangs are quite commonplace. At the moment there are a lot of shootings in the area between rival gangs. When the first gang started basing themselves on the estate to sell drugs and there was the first shooting, everyone was scared of where the situation was heading. A few of the local youth workers met to talk about what could be done, but we were at a bit of a loss as to how to deal with them. Then I thought about the positive impact Kenya had had on Luke, and I suggested that we try taking three of the most influential people in the gang out there to see if they wanted to be involved in something positive. We spoke to the guys concerned and they were keen to go: they'd seen the complete turnaround in Luke's life and it gave them a glimmer of hope that they could do something positive with their lives and influence too. As with Luke and the others who'd come on trips, we raised the money together so it wasn't a handout, but it was also not something that was out of their reach either. The trip completely opened their eyes. We got them involved in a few different projects in Kenya, from just playing football with local street kids to completely refurbishing a house for those street children to live in. Some people thought we were mad taking them, but they worked really hard and didn't cause any trouble. It was a fantastic way to build relationships with them too. We got to see them on a whole different level, and they opened up so much more being away from their usual environment. The fact that we'd invested time in taking them on the trip meant they really began to trust us and our intentions as well.

A number of young people involved in gangs have come on trips to Kenya since then to try to find ways of setting up housing for some of the street children over there. As well as getting them out of their current circumstances for a while, a trip to somewhere like Kenya has a huge impact because it gives young people a chance to help others. Because of their circumstances, they are so often the ones who need something, which can make them feel looked down on. It really empowers them if they can help others and make a difference in their lives. It's incredible to watch them as they see the poverty around them in Kenya. They don't have much themselves, but when they see children running around naked, it gets to them and they start to become even more grateful for what they have got. We've seen gang leaders with tears in their eyes when they're feeding street kids and we know they're going to go home changed. One of the guys, Bugzy, who came out recently, said, 'I never helped no one in my life but now I'm opening up my heart and I've learned how to love other people not just my family. I feel good; it's a life-changing experience.' Another, Louis, commented, 'When you're here you feel like a person who can actually change something. I've never felt that before in my life.'

I think this tactic of targeting the gang leaders and the young people with influence is key. If you find the ones everyone else looks up to and help them make a positive change, you have an opportunity to impact the whole group. That's why we invited a group of twelve guys in whom we saw leadership potential to be part of a mentoring group here at home. All of them have other young people looking up to them and they can use that influence for good or for bad. We offered to invest in them to help them become the people they are meant to be, and they all jumped at the chance. When we started mentoring this group of twelve, none of them were in employment or education, all had been in trouble with the police, two had been in prison and one was an alcoholic. We all go out for dinner together once a month and then we train them to work as volunteers, whether that's doing youth work, helping out at the football clubs we run, or working on our bus that goes out onto the estate. We organise training and talks as well as trips like the one Luke went on, so that they can do something positive and make a difference. Here and abroad they've helped build houses and playgrounds, put on sports days and been involved in music recording, as well as helping build Luke's garage. Now, a year on from when we started, they are all in some form of employment or education and none are in prison. It's incredible to see the change in their lives. I used to see one of them regularly sitting around on the estate drinking a bottle of spirits and now he's got a place at university. Another guy used to rob people in the street and he told me he was heading for prison or an early grave, but he now has a full-time job in a leisure centre.

They all just needed someone to give them some time, give them a sense of purpose and help them make a way for themselves away from their old lifestyles. It's so hard for them to leave the gang lifestyle when their friends are involved and when they can't see any alternative. Some of them aren't willing to change either, and we've learned from experience that there's little you can do until they want their lives to be different. But for most of the guys we know involved in gangs, they don't actually want to stay in that lifestyle. It's messy and they're always looking over their shoulder, wondering who's after them and when they'll need to defend themselves. They want to 'go positive', as they say, but it's hard for them when their gangs are such tight-knit friendship groups and the money they get from crime and drugs is so much more than they can earn with a job. So many of them fall into it when they're young and desperate. For example, one boy we work with grew up with so little money that his mum didn't even have 50p for him to get a can of drink. When he was out with his friends he'd have to spend the whole day thirsty. He had holes in his trainers and there was no food in the cupboards at home. When he was thirteen he realised people were coming onto his estate and selling drugs, offering him £50 just for carrying something across the estate. He could make hundreds of pounds each week and he thought, 'Why not? It will put food in the cupboards.' As he said, it's easy to get into when you're just a kid and you've got older people asking you to do stuff. But then you get older and you're the one recruiting young kids to get involved, and so the cycle goes on.

The key thing is to find positive employment opportunities for the young people who want to change. On one trip to Kenya, one of the guys said to me that he really wanted to change and stop selling crack, but he said, 'What can I do, though? I've got a criminal record so I can't even get a job in Asda.' Another guy we worked with tried to give up selling drugs, but he only lasted a month as he had no other way of making money. He's now serving a five-year prison sentence. Some of the guys are so desperate for work that they don't care what they do, even if they only get the minimum wage and have to work twelve-hour shifts. They sometimes ask for jobs with us and obviously if we know they've just been selling cocaine we can't get them working with young people, but it did get me thinking about training and employment opportunities. Now we're trying to set up a new project called 'Mustard' to create more employment for young people and give them alternatives to drugs and crime. The idea is that local people tell us of any jobs they need doing, whether it's gardening, getting a room painted, having a website built, whatever. We then find a professional to do that job (who gets paid their normal wage), alongside a young person who gets paid £50 for the day. That way the young person can learn on the job, gain experience, earn some money and hopefully find an alternative future. It also provides an opportunity for more people to get involved in kids' lives. Not everyone wants to do youth work, but if you're in employment, the chances are that you could help give work experience and training to someone who's trying to turn their life around.

It would be so easy for people to write off young people like those on our estate, but so many of them want to change and we've found that if you invest in them, they have so much potential. Instead of pointing the finger at people, we need to help them break the negative cycles in their lives. We've become more and more aware that many of the guys we know are having kids really young and, because their own dads haven't been around to spend time with them, we've got this whole generation of young fathers who don't know how to look after their own children. This is a huge problem in our society and a lack of good role models has been shown to be one of the key drivers that pushes young people towards gangs. So we've recently set up a group for young dads on the estate which meets once a month and aims to help them learn what it means to be a father. A lot of it is about having fun and interacting with their children, literally learning how to play with them. We want to do everything we can to break this cycle of fatherless children and help these young guys enjoy time with their kids. We're also running a number of mentoring programmes and have a mobile youth centre we take to six local estates each week to meet and work with more young people. The work that we do could so easily be replicated all across the country, and from our experience you don't even have to start with lots of money, just a genuine passion to help young people.

It's not always easy working with young people, but lots of the teenagers who are working on our projects here and in Kenya are some of the kids we met years ago who had nothing to do but cause trouble. All they needed was someone to love them, care for them and give them a chance to do something positive. For many of them, the world is now full of hope and it's a great feeling when you see a young person completely turn their life around. It does feel as if there's a battle going on for these kids' lives, because they are caught between two worlds. Will they get caught up in gangs, stealing and dealing drugs to make a living and getting involved in all kinds of violence, or will they change and become a positive role model for another young person? I've loved seeing that some of the young people we employ at our mobile youth centre and our football clubs, who used to be getting up to all kinds of things, are now the ones making a difference in their community. They have become role models to others. Often the only role models on estates like ours are the gang leaders who drive around in flashy cars and have loads of money from drug dealing. But if we invest in today's young people and help them do something positive with their lives, they will be the ones the younger kids look up to instead. If any young person who is caught up in gangs or negative behaviour wants to change, then it's up to us to help them get out and be positive. If we work with them, they can become the role models other young people so desperately need. We just need to give them a helping hand and a glimmer of hope that their life can be different.

TRAINING AND EMPLOYMENT OPPORTUNITIES

Ian Levy's story – The Robert Levy Foundation

My son Robert was just sixteen when he was murdered. We are a close family and Robert was always making everyone laugh. He loved sports and was a keen Arsenal supporter. He was such a positive person that everyone liked him. Lots of youngsters are afraid to go into different territories in Hackney, but Robert knew a lot of people (young and old) from various areas and thought no one had reason to hurt him. He was so sure of what he wanted to do with his life. His ambition was to be an architect. We talked about how much work would be involved and how long it would take him to qualify, but he was determined, saying that even after seven years of studying he'd only be twenty-four when he graduated. If his friends at school were slacking, Robert was the one to encourage them to do better. Even the older kids looked up to him and he had a really positive influence on people.

It was a warm and sunny September day when Robert was killed. I was in a meeting at work and didn't check my phone until a break, when I saw my brother had tried to call me a number of times. I returned the call and he told me, 'Someone has been hurt, everyone's saying it's Robert.' I left immediately and don't remember much about driving home other than calling my other two sons to get them to come home straight away. The road leading to the spot where Robert had fallen had been blocked off by the police, but they let me through and I found my son lying on the ground surrounded by paramedics. They had opened Robert's chest and were massaging his heart. They took him to the Royal London Hospital, but it wasn't long until the staff came to see us in the waiting room. They said they'd done everything they could. Robert's brother said, 'He's dead, isn't he?' The nurse nodded and it felt like a whole building was falling on me, crushing my chest. Up until that point I'd been hoping against hope that it wasn't as serious as it looked, but now I knew my son was gone. I rushed out of the room, desperate to see him, but the nurses had already locked the door. Within minutes the police were asking me questions about Robert, wanting to know the names and addresses of the friends he'd been with and the names of everyone who lived in our house. I was so angry, all I could tell them was, 'Go and find the person who killed my son before I do.' I was devastated; crushed. Friends and family were already arriving at the hospital and crowded around in disbelief that Robert was gone.

No one seemed to know what had happened. Robert had never been in any trouble and had certainly not been involved in any violence, so it just didn't make any sense. The friends he'd been with at the time were being questioned by the police, so we couldn't speak to them. We didn't want to leave the hospital until we'd seen Robert. At first the police didn't want us to – they were worried about us contaminating his body for the forensic team – but we had to see our son. He looked amazingly peaceful.

As we came back home that night, I was surprised to see how many people were waiting for us. I felt as if everything was happening through a bit of a daze. People talked to me, but I answered on autopilot without thinking about what I was saying.

Some brought food or made tea, but I couldn't eat or drink. Our extended family moved into the house. They just grabbed sleeping bags and slept on the floor; no one wanted to leave. The community of Hackney was amazing too: they gave us the most incredible amount of support in the days and weeks after Robert's death.

Eventually we found out what had happened to Robert. One of Robert's friends, who lived next door, had forgotten his key and was locked out of the house, so Robert went out to invite him into our home. While they were outside they saw another friend, someone Robert hadn't seen over the summer, so they started chatting and a fourth friend joined them. While they spoke, two boys came up the cycle path and stopped in front of them. One looked at the youngest boy, just fourteen years old, standing with Robert and said, 'What?' They were all surprised, because no one in Robert's group knew either of these boys. The fourteen-year-old replied, 'What?' and with that the other boy took a knife from his sleeve and went towards him. Robert stepped in between them and asked the guy to put down his knife. Instead he stabbed Robert three times – once in the abdomen, once in the neck, and then Robert must have turned to run, because the last wound was where the knife had been driven right through his shoulderblade from behind. The newspapers reported that he was breaking up a fight, but it wasn't even a fight: he was just trying to get the boy to put his knife down.

The boy who did it was just fifteen. He didn't know Robert or his friends and had thought that stabbing someone would help him impress a gang. He went to boast to them about what he'd done, but one of them knew Robert's older brother and was actually on the phone to him at the time when the fifteen-year-old was boasting of his exploits. The boy ran off realising what a mistake he'd made. Later his sister convinced him to turn himself in.

During the trial we found out that he'd hit a teacher with a chair and held up someone with a knife in order to get their mobile phone. The school had received reports that he had a knife in the playground, but apparently nothing was done at the time. With this lack of action and other evidence that came to light during the trial, it was just luck rather than judgement that the school did not have a death on its premises instead of a few yards away. If action had been taken, then Robert would still be here today. Neither the boy's parents nor any other family member showed up in court, even when he was sentenced to life in prison.

Robert's funeral was held at St Mark's Anglican church. It seats 2,000 people, but so many people showed up that some remained standing outside for the service. I remember talking to one of Robert's friends and asking him what he was doing with his life. 'What's the point in being good?' he asked me. 'Robert was trying to help people change their lives and look what happened to him.' It struck a chord with me and I knew we had to do something. All the family felt the same. We wanted to honour Robert's memory and to help young people make positive steps in their lives without going down a road that only leads to destruction and sadness. We never wanted another life to be taken as senselessly as Robert's. We decided to set up a foundation in Robert's name with the aim of helping young people become better citizens. The thing we focus on is keeping young people in education and helping them get training and jobs. As my mum always said, 'The devil makes work for idle hands,' and we knew that to keep young people from gangs and violence we had to help them find positive alternatives.

When a young person comes to us, we try to find out what they want to do and then help them find work experience in that area. We place them with employers who give them genuine experience and not just get them to make the tea. My background is in motor vehicles and my wife's is in fashion, so each year we run summer schools for anyone who is interested in learning more about those areas with a view to them going on to courses in college or university or into employment and apprenticeships. We've teamed up with Hackney College, so we can also offer a course for those interested in working in TV and film. For the course I run, I give the students an introduction to the motor vehicle industry and give them some experience of the different kinds of jobs available. I teach them how to work on cars and fix them up, take them to dealerships so they can see that side of the industry, and also take them to Brands Hatch to see the British Touring Car Championships where they get the opportunity to talk to the mechanics and drivers. Each year we try to expand the course to show them more of the variety of work the industry offers. They also have a project to complete over the six-to-eight-week programme. Previously we had a car donated and we did a *Pimp My Ride* style project, and last summer we assembled a kit car together which we then raffled off at our next annual event.

My wife takes between ten and twelve students on her course, which is suitable for anyone interested in fashion design and textiles. They speak to designers and go on tours of places that produce garments, as well as spending time making some clothes themselves, which are then showcased at our annual event. All our programmes are aimed at anyone who has an interest in any of the subject areas we offer. However, we also aim to reach those who have had difficulties in school or who are involved in the Youth Justice system. We aim to encourage and empower them and channel their energies positively into some new skills and experiences, which we hope will take them into successful careers later in life and away from crime.

The foundation's annual event is held at the Hackney Empire in September, as near as possible to the date of Robert's death.

Ironically, it's the time of year designated as International Peace Week. The event normally starts at 1 p.m. and throughout the afternoon we showcase the talents of local young people, whether that be singing, dancing, poetry or doing a fashion show of the clothes they've made. We invite prominent people from the arts and music industries to come and see the young people. At one of our events, a young lady who had taken part in one of our programmes performed and became one of Guy Chambers's backing singers as a result. All the young people love having the opportunity to perform in the Hackney Empire too. We wanted to do something special to commemorate Robert every year, as well as show the community what the foundation has been doing over the year. The community really supported us after Robert died and, although we can't repay them, we can put on an event that brings everyone together once a year. Every year the event has got bigger and bigger, and this year we had to turn people away as there was no room for everyone despite the venue holding 1,300. One amazing thing is that for a day, everyone is able to put their differences aside. Most of the young people I've spoken to don't even know how or why these stupid postcode wars started, but still they fight each other. It's amazing that at our annual event they can let go of it all, but the ideal, of course, would be that we could somehow make that a year-round thing.

Robert's eldest brother now runs a mentoring programme for children in primary school who are already showing signs of behavioural difficulties. The schools sometimes contact us about children who are already involved or are showing a tendency to get involved in gangs and/or violence and are on the verge of being excluded, which could easily push them further towards getting involved in gangs. The aim of the programme is to develop the individual's self-esteem, communication skills and ability to assert his or her opinions and feelings more effectively and in an appropriate manner. Realistic strategies and advice are given to help young people become successful and motivated individuals. The topics we cover include family, friends and community; strategies to avoid conflict; values and respect; and confidence and motivation. We also give the opportunity for parents to get involved in the programmes, discuss parenting issues and help improve communication at home.

Whenever I'm out, I'll always stop and talk to any young person I see and ask them what they're doing with their life. If they're not in school, work or training, I'll ask what they want to do and how I can help. Usually I end up organising some work experience for them, or get them involved in one of our summer courses. I believe it has to be the responsibility of everyone in the community to help young people, although they must work hard and take some responsibility themselves too. If they want to be helped, we must help them. We can't ask them to leave their gangs and lifestyles without giving them alternatives. If we sit back, the situation won't improve and is likely to keep getting worse.

In the wake of Robert's death, I knew that if I did nothing I would focus on what had happened to my son and that would make me bitter. If I can stop even one youngster from going down the route of the boy who took my son's life, then it's the very least I can do. I want to help channel young people's energy by giving them training and helping them into jobs. It doesn't cost me anything to pick up the phone and help them, but it will cost our community and society as a whole later on if I don't. Who knows, it might even change their life and stop other parents having to bury their child.

If you could provide a positive work placement for a young person, the Robert Levy Foundation would love to hear from you. Please visit their website www.robertlevyfoundation.org *or email* info@robertlevyfoundation.org

THE PRINCE'S TRUST

xl clubs for fourteen-to-sixteen-year-olds

Over the last ten years The Prince's Trust have been running xl clubs in over six hundred schools, usually in areas of high deprivation, working with pupils at risk of exclusion. In the last year alone they have helped almost 13,000 young people.

The clubs run on a two-year programme and are deliberately informal. Between twelve and fifteen pupils take part and meet every week for three hours, when they are guided by an xl club advisor to achieve goals relating to their education, training and future lives. The idea is to re-engage them in education as well as to provide an opportunity to talk about behavioural issues like aggression and attention span. The clubs help young people understand the impact their actions have on other people and enable them to work together with others to achieve a common goal.

Engaging with the clubs helps improve confidence and self-esteem, which in turn increases the number of qualifications the young people attempt to gain. Zoe was one pupil suffering from low self-esteem and was very suspicious of adults. Troubles at home meant she was often unable to concentrate or engage with school and she was predicted to get E and D grades in her GCSEs. Her attendance had dropped to just over 50 per cent and when she was at school, Zoe would often get into trouble with her teachers for her disruptive behaviour. At fifteen she was at risk of permanent exclusion. Through the xl programme, Zoe came to see what behaviour was acceptable and to link her actions to consequences. The support she received from the xl advisors helped her to deal with her problems and focus on learning. As a result her school attendance increased to over 93 per cent and she achieved six GCSEs at grade C and above. She is now taking a year out, working for her family and gaining some work experience before going to college to study English and Sociology.

Team programme for sixteen-to-twenty-five-year-olds

Team is a twelve-week personal development course, offering work experience, qualifications, practical skills, community projects and a residential week particularly aimed at people leaving care, young offenders, educational underachievers and the long-term unemployed. The course includes undertaking a project based in the local community, completing a work placement and participating in a team challenge that involves caring for others.

Dante, aged twenty, from West London took part in a Team programme and found it helped him turn his life around. Having got involved in a gang through his sister's male friends, Dante soon saw how much money could be earned through selling drugs. He started selling cannabis and, aged thirteen, got caught selling at school and got kicked out. He then started selling full time and got involved in a crew. Dante says, 'I liked the superstar status. I became well known and was getting a lot of attention from the girls, which meant more guys heard about you too.' Having met his girlfriend at an exclusion centre, Dante found he was to be a dad just a year later. He says, 'When my girlfriend was pregnant the police were really onto me. My house was getting raided monthly and I was constantly getting arrested. I was on the verge of getting sent down. I had made a lot of money and thought I should count my blessings before I got put away. But I still missed the lifestyle, so I got involved in different types of crime, away from my local law enforcement. I felt like a leader again and got the respect. It was when my daughter turned one that I actually started to realise I was a dad. I started work floor-laying, but wasn't happy with it after a year. I visited a youth worker I knew from before and he told me about The Prince's Trust Team programme.

'I gave it a go and on the programme I got to do work experience at a youth club in the area and really enjoyed it. My girlfriend is a youth worker, but I didn't really know what was involved until then. I spent my two weeks shadowing the manager and so saw all aspects of it – cohesion between different youth clubs, outreach work – I got a taste of everything and really wanted to do it. I started volunteering in a youth club and got my Youth Work Level 1 and 2 VRQ. I was then offered a job with a young fathers' group. When the borough put me on the payroll for that, the youth club offered me a job too. I'm still doing floor-laying, but now looking for full-time youth work. I'm studying for my Level 3 in Youth Work. Next year I want to go to uni and study youth and community with international politics.'

If you would like to volunteer at one of the Prince's Trust programmes, you can find out more on their website www.princestrust.org.uk *or email* getinvolved@princes-trust.org.uk

* * *

Sometimes it is hard to know where to start when you are faced with some of the heartbreaking stories we have encountered in this book. It is easy to feel overwhelmed, but I think the most obvious place to begin is to use your own talent and abilities. Ian Levy's background was in motor vehicles and his wife's was in fashion, so they used their skills to train and reach out to young people. Erin Gruwell's skill was teaching, so she used her classroom to inspire and serve. And as you are about to read, Wizdom from GreenJade used his gift for music to help teenagers influenced by knife and gun crime.

WIZDOM'S STORY

I've always been into music and got into hip hop specifically when I heard the NWA album *Eazy-Duz-It* at the age of eleven. I was pretty lively as a child and spent a lot of time outside the headteacher's office for one reason or another. I looked older than I was (I had a fully grown beard at the age of fourteen) and was used to hanging round with older people as my sister is ten years older than me, so I had a lot of confidence with girls. I always loved parties and was the first person to arrange a disco at my school; any chance I'd get, I'd love to DJ. By the time I was a teenager I was so into music that I made a deal with my mum: she would let me go to under-eighteens raves on a Saturday if I went to church with her on a Sunday.

As a teenager I went to the BRIT Performing Arts School where I got in with a group of guys who were also into hip hop through some DJ workshops. One of them, Keepa, had his own place, so me, CraZee, Rec:A and some of their friends used to hang out there every Friday night watching kung fu flicks, listening to hip hop and freestyling with each other. There were no parents watching us and a lot of the guys were smoking weed, but I was just interested in the music. We were pretty tight as a group and called ourselves the GreenJade Sect – a name we got from a kung fu movie. I got to know one of the guys, Matty, who sold the weed to everyone; he was a taekwondo champion. One day he got robbed and ended up going to court to give evidence against the guy who did it. As a result, a hit got taken out on Matty and a well-known gang wanted to take his life. He started carrying an imitation gun around with him and even a Samurai sword so he could protect himself. The feud was huge, with Matty being chased through the streets by groups holding weapons. The guys in GreenJade felt we couldn't have people chasing him around on our endz; we had to have his back if it came to it. But what happened surprised us all.

Matty was working in the Job Centre as a security guard and one of the women he worked with, June, saw how distressed he was about the situation and asked if she could pray with him. He figured it couldn't hurt, so he started praying with her and over time we began to see changes in Matty. We noticed that he stopped bringing weed when we met up, even though he had been one of the crew's main dealers. Matty was the second loudest member of the crew and you always knew when he was in the house, but we all noticed that he had started to talk about faith, which to start with we all found quite strange. Matty, Rec:A, Keepa, Justin and CraZee had all gone to a Catholic school together and had no interest in Christianity as a result.

One morning Matty made a decision to give his faith a real shot and wanted it to be more than just words or sitting in a church on a Sunday. He wanted it to affect the choices he was making. Later that same day he bumped into the guy who'd robbed him. He was out of prison and couldn't wait to get his hands on Matty to get revenge for his time inside. A scuffle started and Matty was punched to the ground. As a taekwondo champion Matty could handle himself, but he didn't want to fight back as it would have been contrary to his new-found faith. After picking himself up, he said, 'That's it,' and walked away. Because he wouldn't retaliate, the beef was over.

To us, the fact that the feud was over was miraculous – Matty had a hit out on his life, but by taking one blow he'd ended the whole thing. Slowly we began to change as a group and the weed sessions became sessions where we even prayed about stuff, even though we would occasionally get interrupted by one of the guys calling from the police station having been arrested for carrying a knife, as the two stages of our lives overlapped.

We decided to change our names, so Keepa became Wei, Foul Mouth became Logical the Thinker, Rec:A became Judah, Eye Q became 3rd Son and I went from P-Funk to Practical Wizdom. We were still massively into hip hop and were looking for some artists who were putting out positive messages, but there weren't many around so we started rapping over instrumentals and writing our own stuff for our own use, as we felt that we needed to be established in our faith before going out there as a group. We wanted to use our passion for music to reach other kids who were like how we used to be – kids who were sitting around, smoking weed and wondering what life was all about. We decided to keep the name GreenJade, but dropped the Sect as we found new meaning in the words that related perfectly to us. Green symbolises recycling, rebirth, rejuvenation, and Jade (or Jaded) relates to a person of disrepute, so GreenJade – a name we had been using since 1992 – actually meant to be born again.

One New Year's Eve we were at this party with a thousand Christians in Birmingham, but it was so boring. We just felt there was no life to it. That was the same night that Charlene Ellis and Latisha Shakespeare, who were just eighteen and seventeen respectively, were gunned down a few miles down the road. As we drove away from the gig we heard about them on the news and we knew we had to do something about the growing violence among young people.

We wrote a song called 'Gunz Down' about the craziness we were seeing among young people. We really wanted to make a difference in what was happening, but when I talked to a teenager I was mentoring, he very politely asked what difference another song could make. I started to defend my point, but then stopped and listened to what he had just said, and the lights came on. We didn't need another catchy song telling people guns were bad, we needed to meet with the people who were picking up guns and challenge them with an alternative way of resolving conflict.

The point was rammed home to us when we were performing at an anti-gun crime youth event in Clapham. We had done a few songs and were about to perform 'Gunz Down' when a scuffle broke out in the crowd. Security moved in and separated the two groups of youths, ejecting one group while the other was locked inside. It turned out that one member of the group left inside had a knife and was trying to force his way out to finish the fight. Security managed to regain control of the situation as we stood on stage watching. Everything had just about calmed down and we were about to restart the performance when we heard a bang and two masked men (or rather boys) ran into the hall. One of them was carrying a huge silver handgun. They told everyone to get on the floor, but by this time it was pandemonium, with kids running for their lives and screaming. I looked down to the right side of the stage and saw a large group of kids, some as young as eight years old, packed on top of each other desperately trying to hide behind one of the stage speakers. As we were still standing up, mainly in shock and elevated on the stage, the gunman walked up to us and scanned his pistol across us, stopping at 3rd and pointing it at his chest. Thankfully they then fled the scene, having proved the point that they had the power.

I was furious! My initial temptation was to find the people who had put us in that position of fear and hurt them. This, I realised, was a pretty common reaction among the young people too. Someone is held at gun- or knife-point and then they go and get themselves 'tooled up' so they can get revenge, adding to the cycle of violence. I knew we had to help kids who are in that sort of situation to find ways to deal with their emotions and anger.

We spoke to Patrick at XLP who had just come back from doing gangs mediation in Trenchtown. We agreed we had to try to do something pre-emptive for kids aged between eleven and fourteen, as we found that once a young person has joined a gang, it's incredibly hard to get them out of those situations and they have usually made this decision by fifteen. We came up with the idea of a *Gunz Down* show to take into schools, challenging young people that they do have control over the choices they make and that they can talk situations down without having to resort to violence. The show is an hour long and is toured around school assemblies, using drama, music and video to explore the issues around weapons, gangs and making good lifestyle choices.

At the end of most shows we do a Q&A session when the pupils can ask anything they like, and this can be a really powerful time. Because we're outside their day-to-day situation, they can ask us things that they can't ask the other adults in their lives, like their parents and teachers. The show and the hip hop break the ice, help them to believe we've got something to say, and they become interested in what we've experienced. We can share from what we've seen and been through and try to help them learn from our experiences. At one school where we did the show, the pupil group was a bit older than usual, mainly fifteen- and sixteen-year-olds. During the Q&A one boy kept asking us, 'What do you do if someone is standing in front of you with a gun?' We tried to explain that certain actions might lead to that sort of situation, but actually it could be avoided by things like not hanging out with certain people, not picking up a weapon yourself and not getting involved with drugs. The boy just said, 'That's all good, but what do you do if someone's holding a gun to you?' We chatted to him more after the show and realised his life had already reached a certain point where he had to deal with the consequences of his actions so far. In one sense the show was too late to help him avoid that kind of lifestyle. We discovered later that there was already a huge feud with another gang in the area, which was coming to a head. It showed us that even those few school years make a massive difference in terms of the approach you need to take. For the eleven-to-fourteen-year-olds you can try to help influence their mindset, but any older than this and you need to find ways to help them out of the situations they may already be in. You also have to bear in mind that some of the children in UK schools now come from countries that have extreme conflict and violence in their recent history, such as Somalia, Afghanistan and Yugoslavia. You even have children who have been child soldiers, so the issues are really complex and challenging to respond to. For these children and those caught up in violence here, one-on-one help is needed to help them deal with the issues.

The follow-up sessions are a really important part of the *Gunz Down* tour. A team from XLP go into the school to take lessons after the show and that's a time when the issues can be explored in more depth. One time the team went into an all-girls school and during the follow-up the class was asked, 'How do you deal with conflict?' One girl said, 'I cut myself,' to which another replied, 'Me too.' The conversation had started around gun and knife crime, but had opened up to other issues the girls were facing, particularly self-harm. This meant the team were able to discuss other, more healthy ways to deal with pressure and conflict. As a team we realised that gun crime can be just the tip of the iceberg when it comes to all that is going on for young people. We're looking to adapt the show for the future and use it to address a number of issues faced by teenagers today. The aim is still to help them make better choices, but as well as looking at gun and knife crime, we'd like to broaden the appeal to include sexual choices and drug use, as these are also key areas.

Gunz Down was GreenJade's response as a group to the current gang problems. We took what we had (a talent for hip hop) and teamed up with a charity that had expertise in schools (XLP) and came up with the show. But as a society we all need to work out what talents we each have that we could put to good use to change the situation we face as a society. Outside the band I've been involved in parenting classes, which I think are absolutely key in bringing long-term change. First I did the Strengthening Families Strengthening Communities programme with my wife, as we had fostered ten-year-old twins and we wanted some help with bringing them up well. After that we trained to become facilitators on the course and now my wife works with the parents while I work with the young people. I think it's vital that we empower parents to be effective in the world we live in now. I'm sixteen years older than my foster children, but the world they're growing up in has completely changed from the world as it was when I was a teenager, when there was no internet, no mobile phones, no Instant Messaging. One statistic that hits home with me is that 70 per cent of offenders' children become offenders themselves. Children do as they see and not always as they're told. I'd love to involve as many of us as possible with young people and with their parents to stop this cycle of senseless violence.

Gunz Down is now called *Fighting Chance*. For more information, go to www.fightingchance.me

VOLUNTEERING IN PRISONS

Anna's story

I knew I wanted to work with young people in gangs and other desperate situations after something I witnessed while working in South Africa. While I was in a school in a dangerous township where gangs are the norm, I met an eleven-year-old child called

Dylan. He was so lively, funny and brilliant and the group always seemed to revolve around him and the energy he brought to the class. Then he changed, literally overnight. He came into the classroom one morning and didn't say a word at first. Then he began instructing the other children in the manner of someone much older than he was. It was as if he'd gone from being a child to an adult in the space of one day. I asked the school's headteacher about him and she said that the previous evening Dylan had witnessed his dad and his uncle being shot over a drug-related gang incident. Dylan's uncle had died. It was so hard for me to get my head around what that might have been like for him at the age of eleven, to witness such a thing, and it made me determined to do something. I knew there were so many young people in England in similarly desperate situations who felt there was no way out, and I wanted to be there for them.

I came back to the north of England and studied at university to be a primary school teacher, but by the time I left, I knew it wasn't for me. Instead I started doing some youth work and volunteered at a local prison for males aged between fifteen and twenty-one. I had no experience working with offenders, had never been into a prison and had no idea what to expect. When I was taken on a tour of the facility, I was whistled at, spat at and had some unsettling things shouted at me by the prisoners. Some may think that would be offputting but I've learned not to see people for what they do but for who they are. I couldn't make judgements about these guys as I didn't know them yet. After that day I was excited to go back in and begin to get to know them and be part of their lives.

I started going in two days a week and in the mornings would meet with the fifteen-to-eighteen-year-olds and then with the eighteen-to-twenty-one-year-olds in the afternoon. The groups varied each week from as little as two people to up to thirty. We'd play games, talk about different issues and sometimes use the Alpha Course materials to get conversations going, but mainly I just wanted to chat to the lads and see how they were doing. I found that in each new group of lads I saw, there would be some element of the guys testing the waters. They would say really awful things to me, using unsuitable language, ridiculing me about my appearance, or being sexually inappropriate. I'm pretty confident in myself, though, so I would let them know it wasn't right to talk to someone like that and I soon gained their respect. They needed me to draw the line for them: it created a sense of security and trust, which is what those lads desperately needed. If they were unsettled or unsettling others, I always reminded them that I was there on a voluntary basis and they attended the group on the same basis, so if they didn't want to be there they were welcome to go back to their cell. Sometimes they'd get right up close to my face, but I'm six foot tall and I just stood my ground. Some of it seemed like a test, as though they wanted to make sure I could really handle them and the things they'd done. Often, as the group chatted, someone would fly off the handle because they didn't really know how to control their temper or how to act in that situation, but then at the end of the session they'd come and apologise and let me know they hadn't meant what they'd said. They were good lads.

People ask if it was hard for me as a woman to work with male prisoners, but it was important for them to learn that it was possible to have a healthy platonic relationship with a woman. In a prison, often the only women they see on a regular basis are the female prison wardens, who can be quite burly, so sometimes I knew they liked me being there for the wrong reasons. But as we built up the relationships I knew they respected me and the fact that I'm a woman meant they didn't have to compete with me. It also meant they had an expectation that I would listen to them and the things they wanted to talk about.

The truth is, the lads I spent time with in the prison were great and I have a lot of respect for them. I've never met a more genuine group of people and the more I got to know them, the more I knew that if they were just given the chance, they could do awesome things with their lives. My hope in spending time with them was pretty simple – just to build relationships and instil hope in them. The guys just want someone who will sit and listen, someone who will come back week after week and share life with them. They were amazed that I would want to spend time with them, often asking me why I was doing it, assuming I was getting paid loads of money. When I told them I got paid nothing and was volunteering to be there, they were really surprised. It enabled them to believe me when I said I actually enjoyed spending time with them and it helped build the relationships and encourage them that I didn't see them as a project or have an agenda.

Families of gangs

In the north of England you get a lot of kids born into gangs. That might sound strange, but basically there are a lot of old school family gangs and if you're born into that family you have no choice but to be a part of it. Some of them accept it as the way life is; others want to get out, but find there's no support for them. They'd have to move away, change their whole lives and possibly even change their name to be free, as well as needing a whole new family and community to look after and support them. One of the guys told me about a friend of his whose aunt had forced him to smuggle drugs back from Jamaica. After he landed, the drugs didn't pass through his system, so he panicked and went round to his aunt's house. He became aggressive because he was afraid, so she called the police and they locked him up for the night. While he was alone in his cell, the drugs burst into his system and he died of an overdose.

Because of the family connections you do sometimes get whole families in the same prison. For a lot of the guys it's not a big deal being locked up if their brother and cousins are too. In fact for some, they love it. They get food and, if they behave well, a TV and a PlayStation. Most of all, though, they receive love, respect and community and so are genuinely happy to be there. I found it really hard because I wanted them to have a better life, but I understood that it was hard for them to stay out when they couldn't live off the allowance they were given and couldn't get a job. There's so much temptation when they know they can deal or steal to get lots of cash quickly.

Often, people aren't how you might imagine them to be. For example, if you knew someone had committed murder, you might form a grim picture of what they would be like, but I found that was not always the case. I met one twenty-year-old guy who'd been in prison for two and a half years of a twelve-year sentence. I was so surprised to find out he was in for murder – he was so calm, genuine and kind. We used to chat and then one week I asked him what was wrong, as he didn't seem himself. 'Sometimes I get down,' he said. 'Not because I'm in prison; I've learned to deal with that. It's the fact that I have to live with what I've done.' As we chatted more, he told me how one night he'd been in a fight and, with one punch to the other guy's head, he'd killed him. Although they were fighting, he'd had no intention of killing him. 'Every minute of every day it affects me,' he said. 'You can't understand what it's actually like to have taken someone's life.'

Another young guy was from the same area as me, but he dropped out of school before he got to secondary school. He didn't have much of an education, and like a lot of the prisoners he couldn't read, so he ended up just messing around with his mates and getting into trouble. His story was pretty typical – his parents were working all hours just to survive, he was out with his mates getting drunk and doing drugs from a young age. He was involved in a gang and they started stealing cars and bikes in groups, then ultimately he was convicted of GBH (grievous bodily harm). He spoke very little about what had happened, but it was his second stint in prison at the age of twenty.

Volunteering

It doesn't take anyone special to volunteer in prisons. You don't need any qualifications or skills, just the ability to listen and not get easily shocked by people's lives. It's amazing how much difference it can make, too. I used to have this really quiet kid in one of my groups who suffered from depression and would self-harm. The other guys told me he'd been forced into gang activity by his family. He loved it when we played games, though, and one week my team did a music quiz where we played a music clip and the guys had to guess what the song was. One category was theme music from TV programmes and there was this one clip that none of them could guess. Then the quiet lad suddenly jumped up in front of all the other prisoners and started singing the song – which happened to be from *SpongeBob Squarepants* – at the top of his voice! He was completely transformed in that moment from being quiet and troubled to being so confident, and it made me think what a difference something so small can make. After that he really started to come out of himself. The more he could see others were interested in him in a positive way, the more confident he became and the more he opened up.

Sometimes we'd have a brilliant session where the guys would come out of themselves and you could see the changes in them. At other times it was hard and I'd get discouraged – particularly when I'd said goodbye to someone who'd finished their sentence and was leaving prison one week, and then the next week I'd go back and they were already back inside. Some would purposefully break the law in order to be sent back to prison: they thought it was better than the alternative, if that was a difficult family situation or a hostel they'd been sent to. The hostels can often be violent places filled with drug users and drunks, so they figured they'd be better off back in prison with their community in there. For others, though, breaking the law was a habit. One lovely guy I met had been in care since he was young and was in prison by the time he was fifteen. He got out at nineteen and a few days later was walking through a shopping centre. A t-shirt caught his eye, he took it from the hanger, pulled off the tag and walked out with it, even though he had £20 in his pocket and could have paid for it. The security cameras caught him and he could offer no explanation. He said he didn't know why he'd done it, just that the habit was so deeply ingrained. He went straight back to prison.

Sometimes I found the hopelessness of the situation exhausting – especially when it involved guys I thought would manage to stay out and then I'd see them back in prison. I'd start to wonder what I was doing and why I was bothering. But the truth is, there is a value in just being there. The guys I met didn't want me to take on the responsibility of keeping them out of prison, they just wanted me to be a friend to them and be there for them whatever. They wanted people who wanted to spend time with them, not someone who was looking to hit a particular target.

I recently moved to London to work with young people in difficult situations with a view to working with ex-offenders in the future. Prisons are always looking for volunteers to get involved in groups, chat to people and give them some emotional support, and even a few hours a week can make a real difference. I'd love to work with lads and girls who are coming out of prison so they know they are coming out to something. Every person who comes out of prison needs to know that someone is there waiting for them. They need to know that people care about them and will support them. I'd also love to set up schemes for lads so they can train as apprentices and get into work. We are made to have purpose, and if these lads can get a job they are much less likely to end up back in prison, not only because they will have less time to reoffend, but also because they will have something to live for. Of course it's hard for anyone to get employment once they have a record, and often the lads can only get a job by joining a family trade, so I'd love to help them find businesses willing to give them a chance and get them into something they enjoy, whether it's plumbing, building, music or whatever. Anything that gives them purpose and helps them move forward in their lives.

REDTHREAD – WORKING WITH YOUNG PEOPLE THROUGH A&E DEPARTMENTS

Youth charity Redthread partnered with King's College Hospital Emergency Department to start an innovative project with young victims of gun and knife crime. Director John Poyton explains how it came about:

King's College Hospital is one of the largest trauma centres in the UK and is situated near Brixton and Peckham, so the staff see a large number of young people – between the ages of fifteen and twenty-five – each week coming in with stab wounds or after being assaulted. There was a real lack of emotional support for these young people and it would often be the same ones coming in again and again, so we wanted to do something to help them and to reduce the cycle of violence. Redthread had been running a youth clinic in Lambeth for a number of years and together we came up with the idea of the EAR (Emergency Adolescent Room) to target eleven-to-eighteen-year-olds coming into the hospital after assaults.

Because we're working with young people week in, week out, we see trends in the violence. Many teenagers see lots of medical dramas on TV where people get saved from terrible knife wounds, so they think they can stab someone in the leg and the doctors will be able to save them. Tragically, of course, this is not always the case. It appears to be the current trend for people to stab someone in the butt: they're not trying to kill their victim, but leave them needing a colostomy bag so they have to suffer the degradation of the attack for the rest of their life.

Funding only allows for me to be at the hospital for ten hours a week, so I may not be there when the young person comes in, but I follow up with anyone who has come in and has been assaulted. They are given a postcard before they go which has our details on it and then I text, phone or send the patient a letter asking if they want to come back and meet up one to one. Sometimes the parents will respond on their behalf. The young people often deal with the event by trying to put it completely out of their minds, without realising they are possibly suffering from post-traumatic stress disorder. Parents will often say their child has regressed from, say, their fifteen years to acting like a nine-year-old, because that's their way of dealing with what happened. They start to isolate themselves socially and become scared to go out alone, choosing their parents' company over their friends for the first time in years.

The sessions are completely optional and when someone says they'd like some help, we chat to them about having some short-term counselling or mentoring sessions. Rick is a classic example of the kids we see who have low self-esteem that gets them into trouble. I met him when he was about sixteen and he was being brought up by his grandma. He didn't see his parents and had no real male role model. Rick was involved in gang fighting, drugs and robbery and first came to me when he'd been stabbed. We met up to discuss anger management for a while, but he didn't really engage. Then he got his girlfriend pregnant, and at the same time he was arrested and sent to a juvenile detention centre for assault and robbery. I didn't see him for a few years and didn't know what had become of him, but he came back to see me when he was in his early twenties. Out of prison, he wanted to sort himself out, but was aware that his reputation and the things he'd done were still coming back to haunt him. People wanted to fight him over things that he'd done to them or their friends in the past and he had scars all over his body from the different fights and stabbings. Rick was socially isolated and tried to stay out of trouble by staying in his flat, but that meant he was often alone and smoking weed. He got another girl pregnant and the drugs were deeply affecting his moods, making him quite paranoid. With no role models and low self-esteem, Rick is quite an emotional young man. Now he's accessing counselling and trying to work through some of his issues in the hope of turning things around.

We also see people who've got caught up in violence through no fault of their own and are traumatised from being assaulted – people like Marie, who has been assaulted a couple of times in the last few years. The first time a gang of kids from her school thought she was someone else and beat her up. One of the things that Marie found hardest to deal with was that so many kids she'd grown up with on her estate stood around and did nothing during the attack. She is now petrified of going out on her own and doesn't feel safe on her estate, so she is isolated and spends most of her time at home with her mum. The second assault was by someone she thought was a friend. The other girl thought Marie was making moves on her boyfriend and beat her up. Marie needed a safe place to talk and she comes to regular counselling sessions.

Some of the teenagers we see come back to us at different points of crisis in their lives – like Robert, a young man whose father passed away before he became a teenager. He lost his dad and his role model, leaving him with a mother who was suffering from some serious health issues. He came to see us for bereavement counselling and things were going well. Robert was trying to get on, get an education and make something of his life. He didn't want to join any of the gangs on his estate and wanted to stay out of trouble. But one day Robert got mugged and beaten up by a gang. A few weeks later he saw one of the kids involved and pummelled him in retaliation. For the gang, that was it. They said they'd stab him or his mum if he didn't start doing favours for them. Feeling as if he didn't have a choice, Robert started running errands for them at all times of night because he didn't want his mum to know. The 'favours' were things that could get Robert locked up, like moving or hiding guns and knives. Robert ended up back in A&E because of his diabetes, but he engaged with Redthread again because he trusted us from our previous contact. He came away on one of our residential courses, took some anger management sessions and was seen by a mentor. We've seen some great improvements in Robert's behaviour and character over the years, but he is still violent on and off and, to be honest, I don't know which way it will go for him. I've learned that you can't hold on to people or force them to be a certain way. It's so easy for young guys to get swept up into the gang lifestyle – even those like Robert who never intended to be, but feel that their own life and their family's safety is at risk if they don't take part. People like Robert come back and use our services at points of crisis in their lives and I think it's vital that we're there for them when they need us.

Often the young people are feeling incredibly vulnerable when they arrive in A&E and if they are involved in gangs we need to be able to offer them a way out. We're working on partnering with more organisations so we can refer the young people on to get the specialist care they need, whether that's a long-term mentor through an organisation like XLP or getting them back into education through an organisation like Connexions. If they are still in education we talk to their school, who have often already noticed a drop in the pupil's academic achievements around the time of a traumatic event. We also believe it's important to link up with the child's parents (though we have to respect their confidentiality and it's up to them whether they want us to contact their mum or dad). We offer times when a young person can bring in their parents or whole family and talk about issues in a facilitated session. Often at home everything escalates quickly into arguments, so sometimes just having someone else there to help keep things calm really helps. Things get talked about that have never been addressed before and we ask all parties to agree to leave everything in the room and not argue about it once they've left.

We're the only A&E department in the country that runs specific adolescent work, but I think it would be beneficial in any area that is seeing an increase in violence among young people. Ideally we would have someone in the hospital every afternoon and evening so they can meet with each young person as they arrive. As I said, when the teenagers leave the hospital many just want to put the whole thing behind them, so bury it in an unhealthy way. We'd also love to have a building to invite them back to that isn't part of a hospital and therefore seen as part of the state – somewhere in neutral territory where youth workers and health care professionals could see young people under one roof. It would be great to be able to tackle other topics such as sexual health and drug use as well, and underlying factors such as lack of self-esteem. The average teenager doesn't want to walk into somewhere that's just about one thing, as they feel it identifies them as having an issue, so combining everything in one place would be ideal.

Conclusion

If this book has conveyed anything, I hope it is the idea that individuals can make a difference to the lives of young people involved in gangs. In the case of Manny, there was one man who did not judge him but helped turn him around after forty years of violence. Erin Gruwell was one middle-class teacher, but she changed the lives of a whole class and many more. Elijah had a mentor, Chris, who helped him see that he could make something of his life. Miss Lorna, a woman in her fifties, continues to make a huge difference to the lives of gang members in Trenchtown. These inspiring individuals offer young people a sense of purpose, because they know that life without purpose is merely existence. They are all characterised by their ability to listen and then respond to what they hear.

We must not be fooled into thinking that unless we have been around gangs and violence ourselves, we cannot make a difference. If we have the passion we can reach anyone of any social, cultural and ethnic background; the most important thing is simply that we care enough to get involved and that we are consistent. Rather than being paralysed by the scale of the problem, we need to think about what time and skills we could use to make a difference. Robert Levy and his wife are using their knowledge of mechanics and the fashion industry to help young people gain experience, understanding and potential employment; Wizdom is using his love of hip hop; Anna her ability to listen to someone in prison.

What could you use? It could be as simple as helping a child to read, or as complex as setting up employment opportunities like Homeboys. Perhaps you could give time to a local voluntary sector group, or work with local schools to offer experience and apprenticeships in your place of work.

I am not saying it will be easy. In the eighteen years I have been working with young people in London there have been countless times when I have felt that I have wanted to give up because the issues are so challenging and complex. But then I am reminded of the success stories, the lives changed along the way, and these spur me on to try to make a difference and reach those young people who feel they are forgotten.

We can all do something, and we must do something if we are going to give the next generation a fighting chance. I have sat with parents whose children have been killed by gangs and it is hard to convey how helpless you feel in the face of their suffering. For them it is too late; the child they love is gone for ever. I will leave you with one mother's story.

GRACE'S STORY

My fourteen-year-old son David was such a lovely boy, always running up to give me a hug or a kiss, telling me he loved me and asking what he could do to help me in the kitchen. He lit up our house and his three brothers adored him. He was so special and I still sometimes expect to see him coming through the door. He never understood why people got involved in violence. He would say, 'Why do they do this? They should stop killing each other.' He even wrote a speech for a school contest about violence, but two days before he was due to deliver it he was stabbed. These are his words, 'We must not let this teen knife crime take over our culture. I urge you, fight against it. Do not let your child, brother or sister become the next victim.'

David was playing football with his brother in a park near to our home when he was attacked without warning. He was wearing his school uniform and a group from another school considered themselves rivals to David's school. A young boy jumped on him and stabbed him in the chest. David tried to run away towards the main road where he could get help, but they followed him, they wouldn't leave him alone, even then. Running meant he lost a lot more blood, and he fell to the ground.

He struggled for three weeks before he died. I'll never be able to forget the hell of those days. I prayed by his bedside every day that he would survive, but he'd lost too much blood and he had an infection from the dirty knife that was used. I couldn't go back to work for weeks – I couldn't face the reality of life without David.

It wasn't just us, his family, who were affected. David's death shook everyone in the community. I hadn't realised how much people loved David and how much he helped others either, but after he died people were always coming and telling me stories of how he'd helped them carry their shopping, or how he'd walked their dogs when they weren't able to. We gave him a beautiful send-off, but his father and I didn't attend the funeral. We're Nigerian and our tradition is that no parent should see their child buried.

No one should die in the way that my boy did. I go round speaking to young people, telling them what it's like for a mother to lose her son, hoping that they will see sense and stay away from gangs and violence. I will do whatever I can to prevent another child dying like David did and to stop another mother losing a son like I have. There's nothing worse than losing a child.

For more information, go to www.davididowufoundation.org.uk

Appendix A

Advice for Young People

FIGHTING CHANCE

The website at www.fightingchance.me is a new site designed for young people, by young people. It covers the issues raised in this book, features stories of those who have managed to get out of gangs and provides loads of practical advice for any teenager worried about gangs.

Featuring:

- Advice on the complex issues around leaving gangs.
- Music written and performed by young people, expressing the reality of their lives.
- Interactive games.
- Videos exploring consequences of the choices faced by teenagers today.
- Stories of those who have struggled as victims of gang violence.
- Further charities and agencies who can provide more advice and help.

Appendix B

Advice for Parents

HOW DO YOU KNOW IF A YOUNG PERSON IS INVOLVED IN A GANG?

If you are worried that your child or someone you know is involved in a gang, here are some signs that you may want to look out for. While some may be considered 'normal' teenage behaviour, if a number of these signs are present, there is an increased risk that they have become part of a gang.

- Changes in behaviour, such as a young person becoming more withdrawn and distanced from family members, or becoming more aggressive.
- A sudden loss of interest in school/truanting.
- Change in style/dress, for example always wearing a particular colour.
- Unexplained injuries.
- Weapon possession.
- Spending more time with friends (perhaps one group in particular) and staying out later without giving a good reason.
- Using a new nickname.
- New clothes and possessions which suggest an unexplained increase in income.

- Graffiti-style 'tagging' of belongings.
- Use of gang signs and changes in language (increased use of unfamiliar slang).[1]

WHAT CAN YOU DO IF YOU BELIEVE YOUR CHILD IS INVOLVED IN A GANG?

If these signs are present, your child may be involved in a gang and the Home Office offers the following advice.

You will need to talk to your child, but this could be a difficult conversation as they may be scared or unwilling to talk about the situation. For good communication you need to reassure your child that you want to listen and support them. It is also important to be clear that your child does have a choice, even when they think they may not – they do not have to follow the crowd.

Your approach will be more effective if you try the following:

- Stay calm and rational, no matter how upset you are.
- Ask questions, rather than making accusations or rash statements.
- Listen carefully to what they say without interrupting them.
- Really try to understand the situation from their point of view and why they have joined the gang.
- Ask them what you can do to help, rather than telling them what they have to do.
- Point out the risks and consequences of carrying or, worse still, using a gun or a knife (remember that many people who are hurt by guns or knives have their own weapon used against them).
- Try to come up with an agreement on what to do next.
- Work with them to find alternatives to being in the gang.

Finally, there are local community organisations or youth services that can help you. They can offer mentoring, mediation and other ways to help your child leave the gang. Ask at your child's school about the assigned 'safer schools' police officer or community support officer.

TALKING TO YOUR CHILD ABOUT KNIVES

The Home Office also offers the following advice about talking to your child about knives. Think about raising these points with your child.

By carrying a knife, you:

- are giving yourself a false sense of security;
- could be arming your attacker, increasing the risk of getting stabbed or injured;
- are breaking the law.

Not carrying, and walking away from confrontation:

- is what the vast majority do;
- is the tougher thing to do;
- means you will be safer from serious harm and not breaking the law.

Parentline Plus is a national charity that works for and with parents. If you are worried about your child, you can contact them on 0808 800 2222 or visit their websites at www.parentlineplus.org.uk and www.gotateenager.org.uk.

Your local council will be able to advise you about parent support groups and youth services in your area.

You can also find more information on the government's website at www.direct.gov.uk.

Appendix C

Advice for Schools

XLP are running a *Fighting Chance* schools tour using music, film and drama to communicate with pupils about the issues of guns, knives, gangs and making positive choices. You can find out more at www.fightingchance.me. If you are interested in a team coming to your school, please contact XLP on 020 8297 8284 or by email at info@xlp.org.uk.

XLP

If you are interested in finding out more about the work of XLP, or would like to volunteer, donate or get involved in one of our projects, we would love to hear from you. Contact us in the following ways:

Website: www.xlp.org.uk
Postal address: 12 Belmont Hill, Lewisham, London SE13 5BD
Telephone: 020 8297 8284
Email: info@xlp.org.uk

You can also find us on:
Youtube, at www.youtube.com/xlplondon
Facebook, at www.facebook.com/xlplondon
Twitter, at www.twitter.com/xlplondon

Notes

Chapter 1

1. http://www.independent.co.uk/news/uk/crime/cherie-blair-i-fear-for-my-children-858316.html, accessed 29 October 2009.
2. Data from Youth Justice Board Youth Surveys, taken from *Dying to Belong: An In-depth Review of Street Gangs in Britain* (Centre for Social Justice, 2009), p. 20.
3. Street Weapons Commission (Channel 4, 2008), p. 19.
4. http://en.wikipedia.org/wiki/Crips.

Chapter 2

1. T. Bennett and K. Holloway, 'Gang Membership, Drugs and Crime in the UK', *British Journal of Criminology*, 44, no. 3, 2004, pp. 312–13.
2. Street Weapons Commission (Channel 4, 2008), p. 13.
3. John Pitts, *Reluctant Gangsters: The Changing Shape of Youth Crime* (Willan Publishing, 2008), or see www.walthamforest.gov.uk/reluctant-gangsters.pdf.
4. http://www.thisislondon.co.uk/standard/article-23430390-details/London's+gang+wars+claim+the+first+teenage+victim+of+2008/article.do.

Chapter 3

1. http://news.bbc.co.uk/1/hi/england/west_midlands/4270385.stm.
2. *Dying to Belong: An In-depth Review of Street Gangs in Britain* (Centre for Social Justice, 2009), p. 58.
3. http://news.bbc.co.uk/1/hi/england/manchester/3907049.stm, accessed 25 September 2009.
4. Tim Pritchard, *Street Boys* (Harper Element, 2008), p. 92.
5. ibid., p. 135.
6. http://www.guardian.co.uk/lifeandstyle/2008/jul/04/women.ukcrime.
7. ibid.
8. *Dispatches*, 'Rape in the City', Channel 4, June 2009.

Chapter 4

1. *Breakdown Britain, Volume 2, Fractured Families* (Social Justice Policy Group, 2006).
2. Street Weapons Commission (Channel 4, 2008), p. 72.
3. http://www.timesonline.co.uk/tol/news/uk/crime/article4481517.ece.
4. Tim Pritchard, *Street Boys* (Harper Element, 2008), p. 168.
5. ibid., p. 35.
6. *Dying to Belong: An In-depth Review of Street Gangs in Britain* (Centre for Social Justice, 2009), p. 97.
7. World Health Organization figures, as quoted in http://www.independent.co.uk/extras/big-question/the-big-question-why-are-teenage-pregnancy-rates-so-high-and-what-can-be-done-about-it-1623828.html.
8. http://teenagemums.org.uk/the-worst-in-europe.php.

9. Adapted from *Dying to Belong: An In-depth Review of Street Gangs in Britain* (Centre for Social Justice, 2009), p. 99.

Chapter 5

1. *The Culture of Youth Communities*, as quoted in http://www.timesonline.co.uk/tol/news/uk/crime/article 4481517.ece.
2. http://www.telegraph.co.uk/comment/personal-view/3641158/Can-our-broken-society-be-fixed.html.
3. Tim Pritchard, *Street Boys* (Harper Element, 2008), p. 314.

Chapter 6

1. K. Bullock and N. Tilley, 'Shootings, Gangs and Violent Incidents in Manchester: Developing a Crime Reduction Strategy', *Home Office Crime Reduction Series Paper* 13, 2002, p. 28, quoted in *Dying to Belong: An In-depth Review of Street Gangs in Britain* (Centre for Social Justice, 2009), p. 80.
2. *Breakthrough London: Ending the Costs of Social Breakdown* (Centre for Social Justice, 2008), p. 17.
3. Closing the gap in a generation: health equity through action on the social determinants of health (World Health Organization, 2008).
4. http://www.peoplemanagement.co.uk/pm/articles/2009/01/ uk-youth-unemployment-rises-above-european-average.htm.
5. *Breakthrough London: Ending the Costs of Social Breakdown* (Centre for Social Justice, 2008), p. 10.
6. http://www.cinematical.com/2007/01/06/interview-freedom-writers-erin-gruwell-jason-finn-and-maria-r/, accessed June 2009.
7. Street Weapons Commission (Channel 4, 2008), p. 73.

Chapter 7

1. *London Paper*, 3 January 2008, from Claire Alexander, *(Re)Thinking 'Gangs'* (Runnymede Trust, 2008).
2. http://news.bbc.co.uk/newsbeat/hi/the_p_word/newsid_8119000/8119417.stm, accessed 29 June 2009.
3. www.timesonline.co.uk/tol/news/uk/article431424.ece?token=null&offset=0&page=1.
4. www.timesonline.co.uk/tol/news/uk/crime/article3981141.ece.
5. http://www.timesonline.co.uk/tol/news/uk/article3446273.ece.
6. John Pitts, *Reluctant Gangsters: The Changing Shape of Youth Crime* (Willan Publishing, 2008), also accessed at www.walthamforest.gov.uk/reluctant-gangsters.pdf.
7. Martina Cole, *Girls in Gangs* (Sky TV, 2009).

Chapter 8

1. Greg Paul, *The Twenty-Piece Shuffle* (David C. Cook Publishing, 2008).

Chapter 9

1. *Dying to Belong: An In-depth Review of Street Gangs in Britain* (Centre for Social Justice, 2009), p. 69.
2. ibid., p. 92.

Chapter 10

1. *Dying to Belong: An In-depth Review of Street Gangs in Britain* (Centre for Social Justice, 2009), p. 198, taken from RAND Corporation study.
2. Street Weapons Commission (Channel 4, 2008), p. 66, which references *The Economic and Social Costs of Crime against Individuals and Households 2003–04* Home Office, June 2005.

3. Study conducted by the Department of Psychology at Goldsmiths, University of London, ongoing since October 2006.

Appendix B

1. Adapted from *Gangs: You and Your Child* (Home Office).